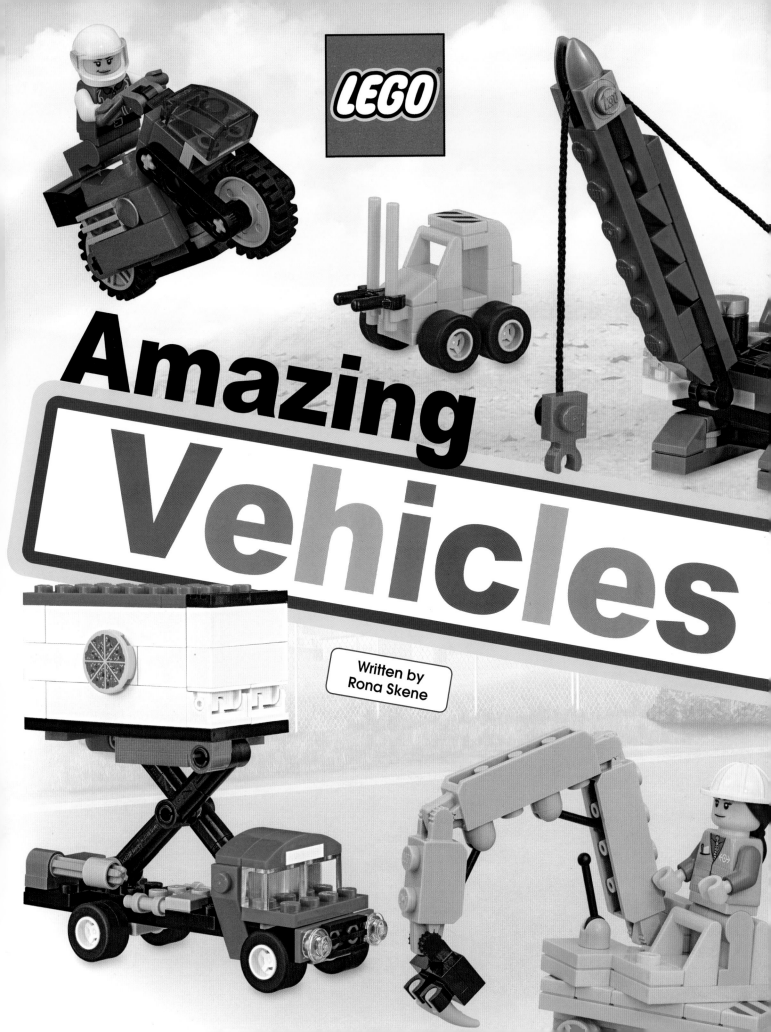

LEGO®

Amazing Vehicles

Written by
Rona Skene

 | Penguin Random House

Senior Editor Tori Kosara
Project Art Editor Jenny Edwards
Design Assistant James McKeag
Pre-Production Producer Siu Yin Chan
Producer Louise Daly
Managing Editor Paula Regan
Managing Art Editor Jo Connor
Art Director Lisa Lanzarini
Publisher Julie Ferris
Publishing Director Simon Beecroft

Inspirational models built by Jason Briscoe, Barney Main, and Simon Pickard
Vehicles consultant Phil Hunt
Builds consultant Simon Hugo
Photography by Gary Ombler

Dorling Kindersley would like to thank Randi Sørensen, Heidi K. Jensen, Paul Hansford, Martin Leighton Lindhardt, Melody Louise Caddick, Charlotte Neidhardt, and Ulla W. Pelsø at the LEGO Group; and Kayla Dugger at DK for Americanizing.

First American Edition, 2019
Published in the United States by DK Publishing
1450 Broadway, Suite 801, New York, NY 10018

A catalog record for this book
is available from the Library of Congress.
ISBN 978-1-4654-8261-7

Printed and bound in China

**A WORLD OF IDEAS:
SEE ALL THERE IS TO KNOW**

www.LEGO.com
www.dk.com

Contents

Turn to page 66 to find the building instructions for these four models!

How vehicles go

There are so many ways to travel, but how do vehicles get moving? Each mobile machine needs someone or something to give it force to move. Engines, wind, and even people can provide the energy needed to make cars, boats, bicycles, and more go.

Timing chain turns camshaft to open intake valves

Intake valve lets air and fuel into the chamber

Camshaft

Chamber where fuel and air mix, causing little explosions and creating pressure to move the pistons

Piston inside moves up and down and turns the crankshaft

Connecting rod

Crankshaft collects power from the moving pistons to make the vehicle's wheels move

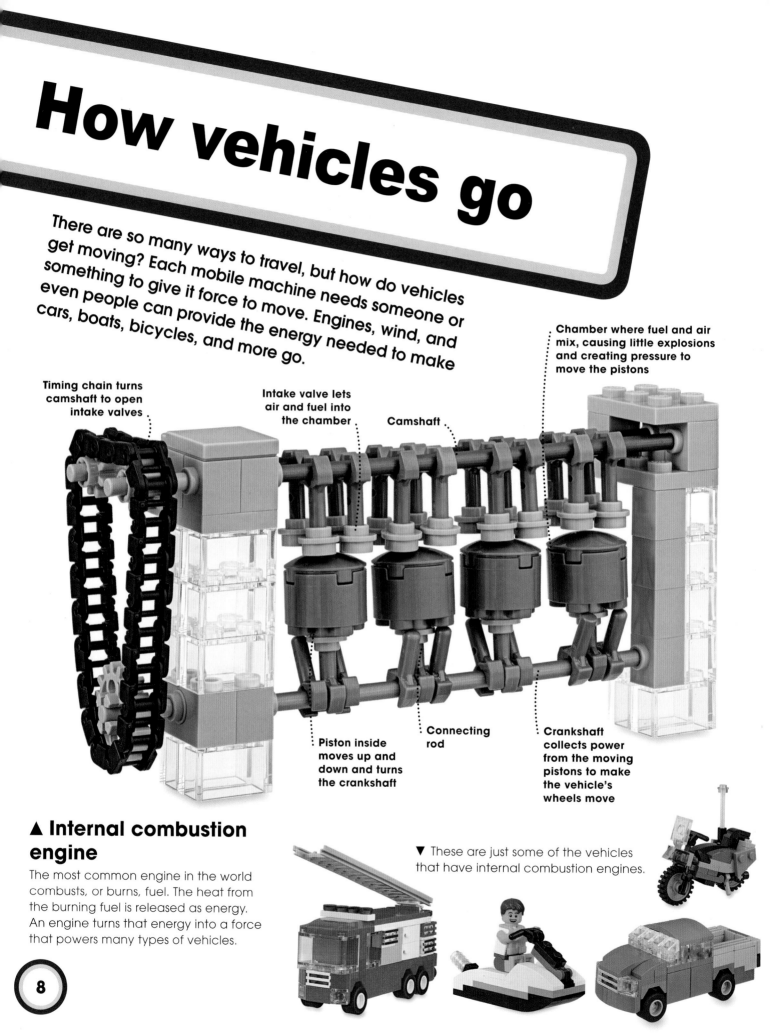

▲ Internal combustion engine

The most common engine in the world combusts, or burns, fuel. The heat from the burning fuel is released as energy. An engine turns that energy into a force that powers many types of vehicles.

▼ These are just some of the vehicles that have internal combustion engines.

Jumbo jet

▲ Jet engine

A jet engine works much like an internal combustion engine does. However, jet engines burn fuel and air constantly instead of in little explosions. This means jet engines have more power and can make planes fly at super speeds.

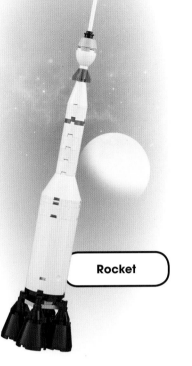

Rocket

▲ Rocket engine

A rocket engine is a type of powerful jet engine. Because there is no air in space, rockets cannot use air from the outside to burn fuel like normal jet engines. Instead, they carry air with them in tanks filled with oxygen.

Hot air balloon

▲ Hot air

A flame underneath the balloon's fabric, called the envelope, heats up the air inside the balloon. Hot air is lighter than cold air, so the warm air in the envelope lifts the balloon into the surrounding cooler air.

Trading ship

▲ Wind power

Wind can be a powerful force. Some vehicles, such as trading ships, capture the energy of the wind and use it to push the vehicle forward.

Steam train

▲ Steam power

Steam trains are powered by heating up water. Boiling water produces steam, which pushes pistons that then turn the wheels of a vehicle, such as a train.

I'M USING PEDAL POWER!

Penny-farthing

▲ People power

Before engine and animal power, people moved vehicles by pulling, pushing, pedaling, or paddling. Some vehicles, such as bicycles and kayaks, are still powered by human beings.

Horse-drawn mine cart

▲ Animal power

Animals can provide force by pulling vehicles to make them move. Horses, oxen, and dogs often helped to pull carts, plows, sleighs, and more before engines were invented.

Minivan

▲ Electricity

Electric vehicles rely on batteries to power their motors instead of fuel. The batteries are charged by plugging a cable connected to the vehicle into a socket, just like a lamp.

To the rescue!

When there's trouble, emergency vehicles take to the sky, water, or road to save the day. These machines have the speed and all the equipment needed to help in difficult situations.

▼ Fire engine

Speedy fire engines race to rescue burning buildings. Fire engines carry a crew of firefighters, as well as tools and hoses to put out the blaze.

Ladder extends to reach tall buildings

Hoses stored in rear

Fire crew sit in the jumpseat

Storage compartment for firefighting tools

Emergency lights

Locker for storing emergency equipment

◄ Ambulance

Flashing lights and a loud siren tell traffic to move out of the way when an ambulance is carrying a sick or injured passenger to the hospital. There is room for a stretcher and medical equipment in the back.

Engine compartment

Flashing light

Windshield

Pannier holds police equipment

Headlamp

Kickstand for parking

Record breakers

The **fastest fire engine** is jet-powered! The engine, named the *Hawaiian Eagle*, has a top speed of 407 mph (655 kph).

The **highest helicopter rescue** ever took place 4 miles (7 km) up a mountain in Nepal. Three stranded climbers were rescued.

▲ Police motorcycle

These fast bikes can weave around other vehicles on the road to get to an emergency quickly.

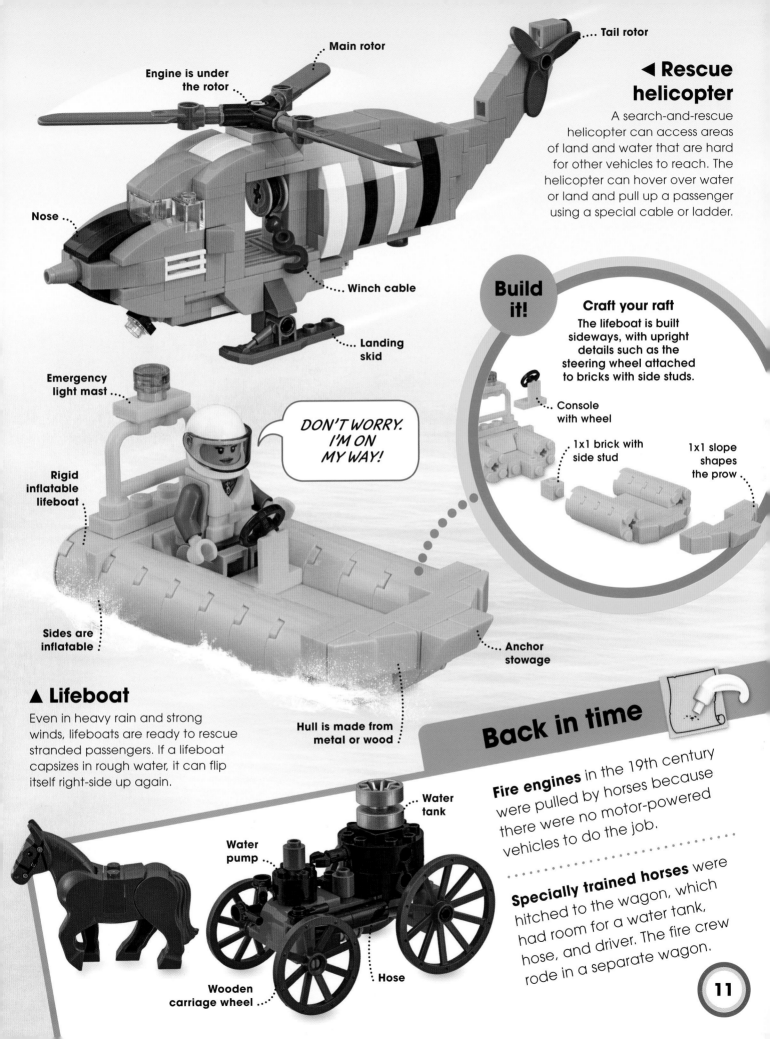

Rescue helicopter

A search-and-rescue helicopter can access areas of land and water that are hard for other vehicles to reach. The helicopter can hover over water or land and pull up a passenger using a special cable or ladder.

Engine is under the rotor

Main rotor

.... Tail rotor

Nose ....

Winch cable

Landing skid

Emergency light mast ....

DON'T WORRY. I'M ON MY WAY!

Rigid inflatable lifeboat .

Sides are inflatable .

Build it!

Craft your raft
The lifeboat is built sideways, with upright details such as the steering wheel attached to bricks with side studs.

Console with wheel

1x1 brick with side stud

1x1 slope shapes the prow

Anchor stowage

Hull is made from metal or wood

▲ Lifeboat

Even in heavy rain and strong winds, lifeboats are ready to rescue stranded passengers. If a lifeboat capsizes in rough water, it can flip itself right-side up again.

Back in time

Fire engines in the 19th century were pulled by horses because there were no motor-powered vehicles to do the job.

Water tank

Water pump ....

Specially trained horses were hitched to the wagon, which had room for a water tank, hose, and driver. The fire crew rode in a separate wagon.

Hose

Wooden carriage wheel ...

11

At the building site

Tough building work calls for mobile machines with strength and durability. Mighty construction vehicles lift, haul, dig, and roll at busy building sites to help make buildings and roads.

Backhoe loader ▼
This versatile vehicle can be fitted with different tools to dig or break the ground. At the other end, a scoop carries earth and rubble.

Loader bucket

Concrete slides out of a chute at the back

Spinning drum

Jackhammer to break ground

Swing frame

▶ Concrete mixer

Inside the mobile mixer's spinning drum, cement is churned with water to keep it fluid. After the mixture is poured out, it sets to form hard concrete.

ALL THIS SPINNING IS MAKING ME DIZZY!

Mix it up with LEGO® Technic

The two halves of the mixer's drum slide onto a LEGO® Technic axle, which pivots on a long LEGO Technic peg.

LEGO Technic cross axle

Long LEGO Technic peg

LEGO Technic cross block

1x1 brick with hole

Build it!

Exhaust pipe

Driver-operated levers control the bulldozer

▶ Bulldozer

With its huge metal blade, a bulldozer easily clears the way through heavy earth and rocks. Continuous tracks enable it to drive over rocky and soft ground.

Blade can lift and tilt

Continuous track

String with two studs ...

Create a crane
The crane's cab rotates on a 2x2 turntable piece. The cable is a string with studs that rests on a hinged jib.

2x2 turntable

Jib .

Record breakers

The **strongest crawler crane** lifts 300 tons (272 tonnes). That's about the same weight as 150 cars!

The **biggest bulldozer** had such a long blade, that four adult men could lie down end-to-end in it.

◀ Crawler crane

This handy vehicle lifts heavy loads. Crawler cranes roll slowly across building sites on tracks to transport their loads.

Tracks keep the crane steady on all types of terrain

Driver's cab

Drum roller

Hook is raised and lowered on a strong cable

Engine is at the back of the vehicle ....

▶ Dump truck

Wide dump trucks carry rocks, sand, or earth around the building site. A big engine powers a hydraulic lift, which tilts the truck bed so that the load is emptied out.

Load is carried in the open bed

▲ Road roller

A road roller's massive, drum-shaped wheels are super-heavy. They can flatten earth or smooth out the surface of a newly laid road.

Cab windows keep the dust out ...

THIS TRUCK ROCKS!

· Hinge

On the racetrack

Speeding around a track, zipping through the air, or zooming down the ice, racing is fun. Each racing machine is different, but they are all built with one thing in mind—speed!

Build it!

Art of the kart
Combine small silver or gray parts at the back of the kart to make a complex-looking motor.

Gray tap piece

Record breakers

In 2010, Michael Pfister set the **world record** for luge speed at 96 mph (154 kph). That's faster than the average speed of a car.

The **world's first motor race** was held in France in 1894. It took the winning driver nearly seven hours to finish the 79-mile (127-km) course.

HEY, WAIT FOR ME!

Space for only one person

Body is close to the ground

Front bumper

▲ Go-kart
Small, swift go-karts race on twisted tracks. Most go-karts have soft tires that grip the track better than normal tires for more control.

WHAT AN "ICE" RIDE!

Tight-fitting bodysuit

Luges have no brakes—racers use their feet to stop

▶ Luge
This racing sled is called a "luge," which means "sled" in French. The rider lies flat on his or her back and pushes the luge forward to speed down an icy track.

Steel is the only part of the luge that touches the ice

Short fin helps the plane go faster

Carbon-fiber body makes the plane light and fast

◄ Racing plane

Air racing is not just about speed. Planes perform tricky turning maneuvers, too. The planes are super-light, and their smooth, sleek shape is designed to cut through the air easily.

Landing wheels are covered so air flows smoothly around them

Secrets of spin

The plane's propeller slots onto a bar, with a 1x1 ring to hold it in place. Don't secure the propeller too tightly if you want it to spin around.

Bar piece

2x2x2 cone

Propeller piece

1x1 round plate with hole

Spoiler streamlines the shape so car goes faster

Build it!

Stripes help viewers identify the car at high speeds

▲ Race car

Whether it's blazing around a track or a long-distance rally, car racing has been popular since the first motor vehicle was invented. Race cars are made for maximum speed and are driven by highly skilled drivers.

Smooth tire

Back in time

Ancient Roman chariot races were fast and furious! Driven by one man and **pulled by horses**, chariots raced around oval-shaped racetracks.

Racing chariots had two wheels and were made of wood or wicker. They were light and maneuverable to get around tight bends.

Carriage was open at the back

Charioteers competed standing up

Sometimes multiple horses pulled a chariot

Around the city

Cities are filled with vehicles traveling from place to place carrying passengers or goods. There are so many ways to get around busy city streets. With ice cream truck music and vehicle horns, there is plenty of noise, too!

Record breakers

Melbourne, Australia has the world's **biggest city tram network**, with around 500 trams and more than 1,700 stops.

In Brazil, the **world's longest bus** has three sections connected by pivoting joints. It's about the same length as six family cars.

Ice cream machine

Loudspeaker plays music

Serving hatch

Ice cream truck ▲

The ice cream truck plays a cheerful chiming song to let everyone know that sweet treats are on the way. Built-in freezers keep frozen treats cool, even on a hot summer day.

THIS IS THE COOLEST TRUCK IN TOWN!

Handlebars for steering

◄ Tricycle

Riding through the city park on a tricycle is fun. With three wheels, it's easier to stay balanced on a tricycle than on a two-wheeled bike.

Two back wheels help balance the tricycle

Single front wheel

Roof can be folded down

Room for two passengers

Auto rickshaw ►

These small passenger carriers are great for zipping through busy and narrow urban streets. They are designed for short journeys.

Open sides

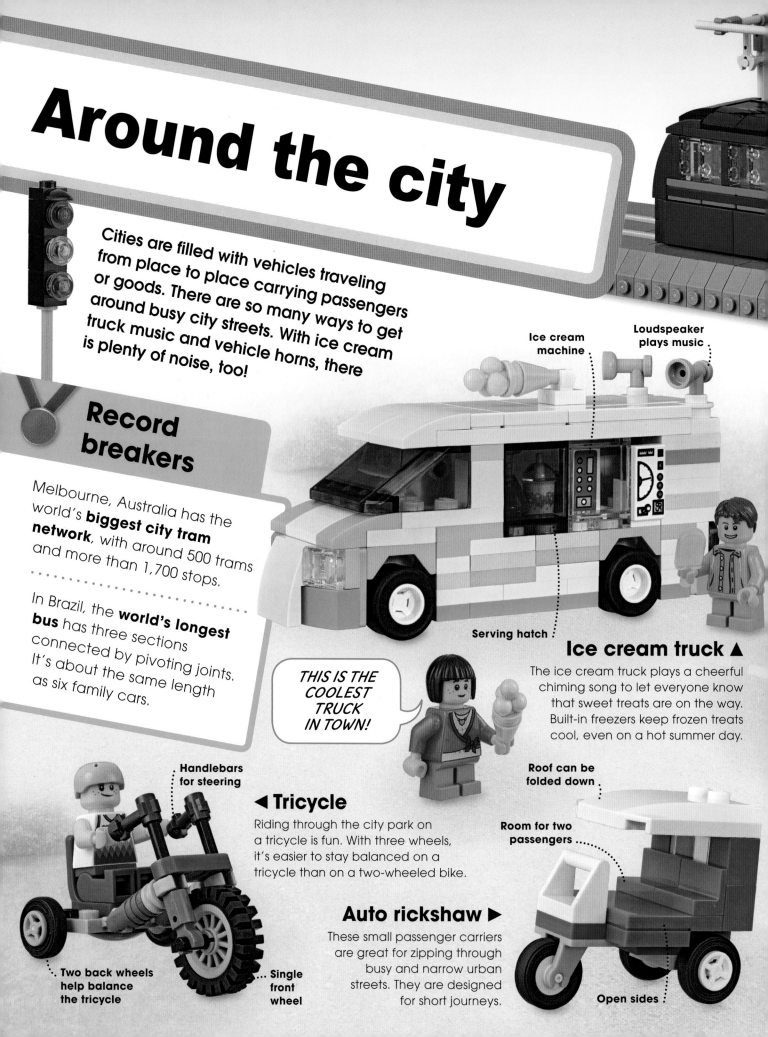

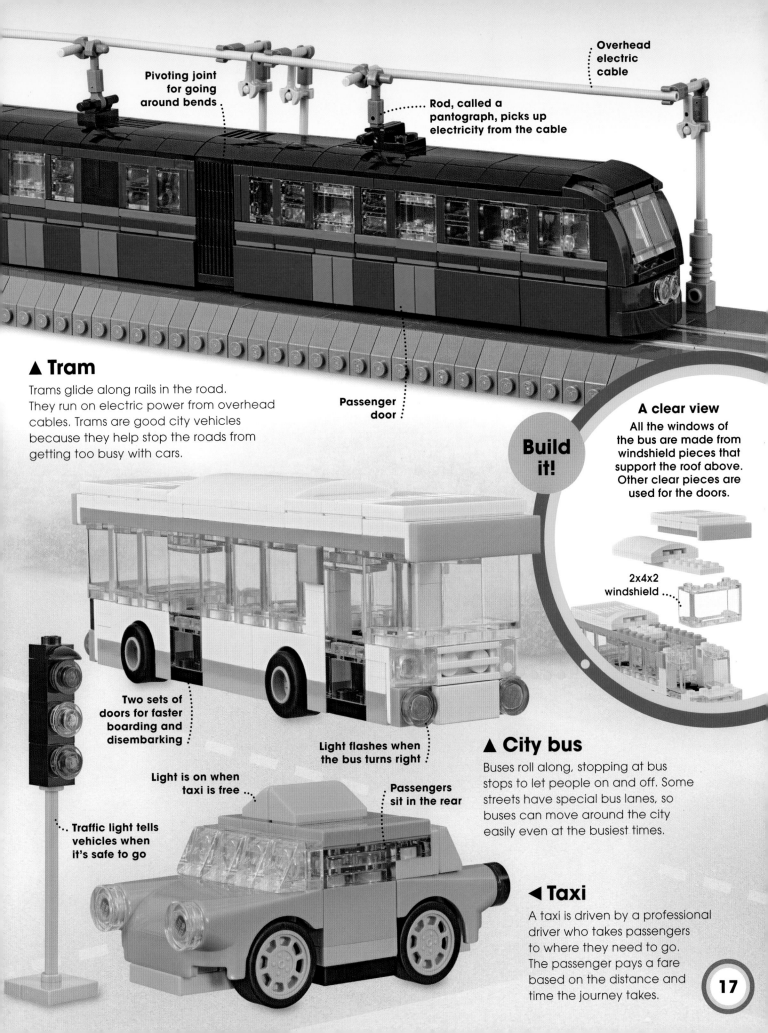

Pivoting joint for going around bends

Rod, called a pantograph, picks up electricity from the cable

Overhead electric cable

▲ Tram

Trams glide along rails in the road. They run on electric power from overhead cables. Trams are good city vehicles because they help stop the roads from getting too busy with cars.

Passenger door

Build it!

A clear view
All the windows of the bus are made from windshield pieces that support the roof above. Other clear pieces are used for the doors.

2x4x2 windshield

Two sets of doors for faster boarding and disembarking

Light flashes when the bus turns right

▲ City bus

Buses roll along, stopping at bus stops to let people on and off. Some streets have special bus lanes, so buses can move around the city easily even at the busiest times.

Light is on when taxi is free

Passengers sit in the rear

Traffic light tells vehicles when it's safe to go

◄ Taxi

A taxi is driven by a professional driver who takes passengers to where they need to go. The passenger pays a fare based on the distance and time the journey takes.

Rolling through time

When humans put wheels on the first cart, they could never have guessed what would happen next! For thousands of years, the invention of the wheel has made all kinds of vehicles possible—from a simple bicycle to a car that drives itself.

An axle fits through the hole to join the wheel to a cart

3500 BCE
Wheels
Before they helped vehicles roll along, wheels were used to help potters make pots. Three hundred years after these were invented, lighter wheels were attached to chariots.

Early wheels were solid disks of wood

1860s
Steam tractors
Steam-powered tractors replaced horses for heavy farm work. They were useful but were eventually replaced by smaller, more affordable gas-powered tractors.

Driver's seat

Flywheel powered a machine to separate grain from wheat

1920s
Family cars
The first gas-powered car was made in 1886, and it changed the way people traveled. By the 1920s, factories worldwide produced millions of affordable, reliable cars for families to use.

Early cars often had open tops

Wheels were made of wood

.... Each driver chooses a colorful theme

1980s
Monster trucks
Early monster trucks were modified pickup trucks with huge wheels. They appeared in special races and shows.

Giant tires for stunts

2010s
Self-driving cars
Computers started driving cars in the 21st century. Cameras and sensors on a car send data to a computer, enabling the vehicle to steer around obstacles and operate safely.

Sensor scans the area to keep the vehicle safe

Camera

Build it!

Full steam sideways!
The steam car is built around a sideways angle plate, with 1x1 round plates for wheels built onto bricks with side studs.

Bar secures lid on barrel

1x1 headlight brick

1x2/2x2 angled plate

1x1 brick with two side studs

I'M READY TO ROLL!

1760s
Steam-powered cars
The earliest road cars were steam-powered carriages. They were slow, and their heavy steam boilers had to be refilled with coal every 15 minutes.

Boiler

Throttle lever controlled speed

Tiller for steering

1810s
Bicycles
The first-ever bicycle was known as the "dandy horse." It had no pedals. To move the wheels, the rider sat on the saddle and walked or ran on the ground.

Saddle

Wooden frame

1950s
Flying cars
These amazing vehicles were plastic cars with detachable wings, a propeller, and a tail. They could convert from road to flight mode in just a few minutes.

Folding wings

Room for driver and one passenger

1970s
Hydraulic excavators
Until the 1970s, most diggers used wire cables to move the boom. The invention of hydraulics allowed fluid inside the machine to power the boom instead. This made excavators more powerful.

Bucket

Boom

Continuous track

Wings and wheels
The wheels of the flying car are 1x1 round tiles on LEGO® Technic half pins in plates with rings beneath.

LEGO Technic half pin

1x1 round tile

2x2 plate with rings beneath

Build it!

19

Underneath the ground

Most vehicles travel above ground—on land, on water, or in the air. But some vehicles are specially made to move people or do important jobs under the Earth's surface.

THIS LOADER IS "MINE"!

Scoop

Flat body for low ceilings

Tough tires are hard to puncture

Mine loader ▲

Specialized trucks help mine-workers move coal and rocks deep underground. Designed to operate in cramped spaces, the trucks are low and easy to drive through narrow spaces.

Record breakers

Beijing, China is home to the **world's busiest subway system**. It carries almost 10 million passengers every day.

The **biggest roadheader** in the world weighs a ground-crushing 135 tons (122 tonnes)—the same as 20 African elephants!

Passenger carriage

Large windows

▲ Subway train

In some big cities, the quickest transportation network is hidden under the street. Subway trains travel through a network of tunnels, bypassing the traffic and crowds on the streets above.

Train operator's cab

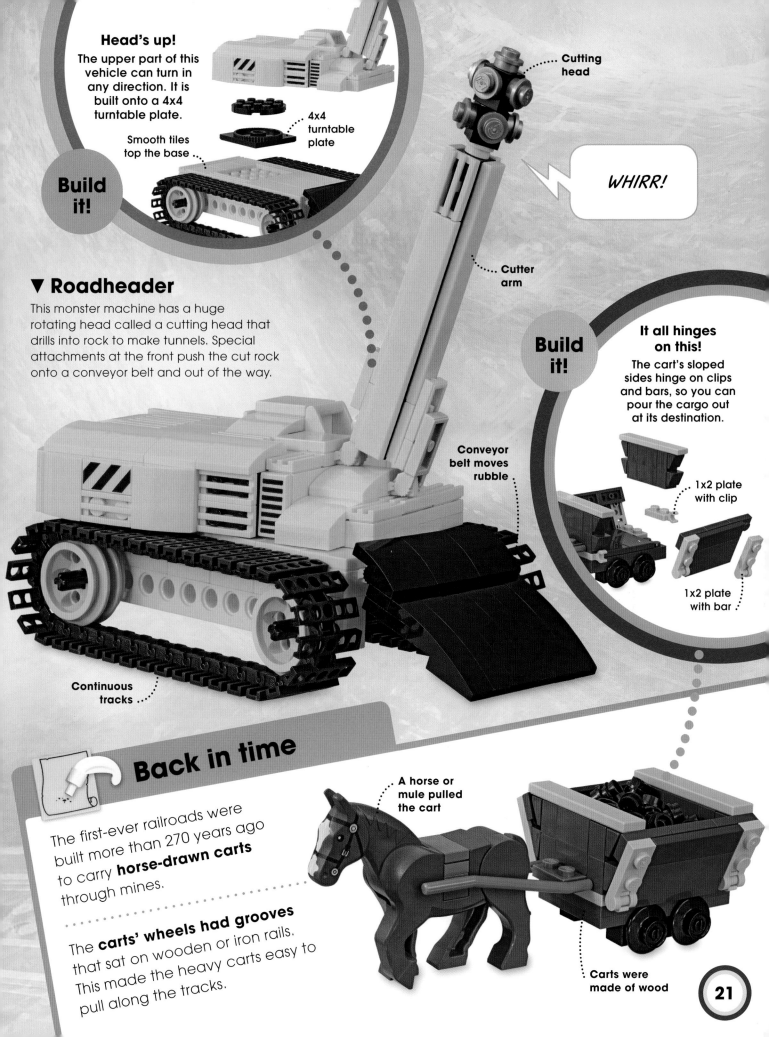

Head's up!
The upper part of this vehicle can turn in any direction. It is built onto a 4x4 turntable plate.

Smooth tiles top the base

4x4 turntable plate

Build it!

Cutting head

WHIRR!

Cutter arm

▼ Roadheader
This monster machine has a huge rotating head called a cutting head that drills into rock to make tunnels. Special attachments at the front push the cut rock onto a conveyor belt and out of the way.

Build it!

It all hinges on this!
The cart's sloped sides hinge on clips and bars, so you can pour the cargo out at its destination.

Conveyor belt moves rubble

1x2 plate with clip

1x2 plate with bar

Continuous tracks

Back in time

The first-ever railroads were built more than 270 years ago to carry **horse-drawn carts** through mines.

The **carts' wheels had grooves** that sat on wooden or iron rails. This made the heavy carts easy to pull along the tracks.

A horse or mule pulled the cart

Carts were made of wood

Down at the docks

At the docks, boats and ships carry goods in and out of the harbor. Land vehicles then help move the goods from sea-going vessels to stores and warehouses.

Towboat has a flat front to push the barge

Shipping container

Wide, flat shape helps it to float even when filled with heavy cargo

▲ Barge

Barges have flat bottoms and wide decks to carry heavy loads of goods along rivers and canals. Most barges are pushed by towboats or pulled by tugboats.

Build it!

A tow in the water
The tug's towline is a drum piece on a LEGO® Technic axle. Bricks with holes hold it in place but still allow it to turn.

LEGO Technic 1x2 brick with hole

String winds onto the drum

LEGO Technic axle

Drum

Mainmast

Steel towing rope

Reel

Tugboat ◀

In a crowded port, it's not easy for big ships to maneuver, but powerful tugboats can. Using a strong towline, tugboats pull larger ships to where they need to be.

Hull made of steel

HOOONK!

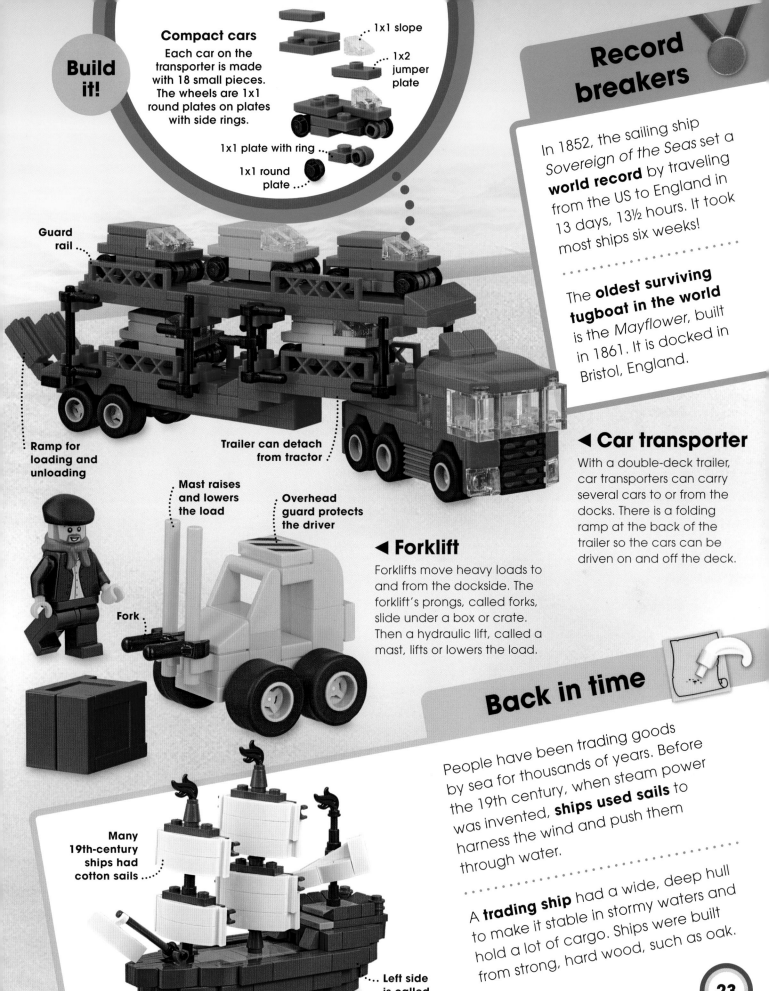

Compact cars

Each car on the transporter is made with 18 small pieces. The wheels are 1x1 round plates on plates with side rings.

1x1 slope

1x2 jumper plate

1x1 plate with ring

1x1 round plate

Record breakers

In 1852, the sailing ship *Sovereign of the Seas* set a **world record** by traveling from the US to England in 13 days, 13½ hours. It took most ships six weeks!

The **oldest surviving tugboat in the world** is the *Mayflower*, built in 1861. It is docked in Bristol, England.

Guard rail

Ramp for loading and unloading

Trailer can detach from tractor

◀ Car transporter

With a double-deck trailer, car transporters can carry several cars to or from the docks. There is a folding ramp at the back of the trailer so the cars can be driven on and off the deck.

Mast raises and lowers the load

Overhead guard protects the driver

◀ Forklift

Forklifts move heavy loads to and from the dockside. The forklift's prongs, called forks, slide under a box or crate. Then a hydraulic lift, called a mast, lifts or lowers the load.

Fork

Back in time

People have been trading goods by sea for thousands of years. Before the 19th century, when steam power was invented, **ships used sails** to harness the wind and push them through water.

A **trading ship** had a wide, deep hull to make it stable in stormy waters and hold a lot of cargo. Ships were built from strong, hard wood, such as oak.

Many 19th-century ships had cotton sails

Left side is called port side

23

In the water

Most of the planet is covered with ocean, so there are plenty of vehicles made to travel through water. Watercraft carry people and goods all over the world.

Pilot house

Struts to keep the craft stable

Front foils

Rear foils

▲ Hydrofoil

A hydrofoil skims above the water on foils. As the boat speeds up, the foils lift it clear of the waves. With less drag from the water, the craft can move at fast speeds.

Make it shipshape

Build the sides of the ship's hull separately, then attach them using bricks with side studs.

Build it!

Five 1x2 bricks with two side studs

1x2 curved slope

Porthole

Lifeboat

Swimming pool

Cruise ship ▲

These floating hotels take tourists on fancy trips to vacation destinations. Some ships are so big, they are like mini-cities—with restaurants, movie theaters, and stores.

Thruster propels the craft forward

Thick-walled window

◀ Submersible

Scientists use submersibles to explore and map the underwater world. These tough craft are specially designed to withstand the pressing weight of deep water.

Robotic arm

Radio antenna

Wheelhouse is the captain's control center

Exhaust pipe

▲ Fishing trawler

Fishermen and women use these boats to fish all over the world. The boats help catch and carry seafood, such as fish and crab, and take it back to shore.

Buoy for docking

Refrigerated hold keeps seafood fresh while at sea

Record breakers

English rower John Fairfax was the **first person** to row alone across the Atlantic Ocean in 1969. It took him six months.

In 2012, the submersible *Deepsea Challenger* reached **the deepest point on Earth** in the Pacific Ocean.

ROW, ROW, ROW YOUR BOAT . . .

Rowboat ▶

A rower uses a pair of oars to power a rowboat. As the rower pulls the oars through the water, the force pushes the boat forward.

Oar is flat at one end

Rowlock keeps the oar in place

One brick, two windows

Use headlight bricks as micro-scale portholes, or turn them around to make square windows.

1x1 headlight brick

1x1 headlight brick

Build it!

Back in time

In the 19th century, the **steamboat** was the fastest boat on the water.

It was powered by a steam engine that **drove a large wheel**. As it turned, the wheel's paddles pushed through the water, moving the boat forward.

Funnel

Paddle wheel

Paddle blade

Sailing through time

Traveling on or under the water has been an important way to get around for thousands of years. From ancient log canoes to vast, floating vacation villages, cruise through the long history of water vehicles.

Around 8000 BCE
Dugout canoes
Thousands of years ago, humans made simple canoes from logs. Stone Age fishermen cut down and hollowed out the tree trunks with sharpened flint rocks.

Canoes were made from wood, such as linden ...

Room for up to eight people

800s CE
Viking longships
The Vikings built ships to take them long distances from their home in Scandinavia. These boats could operate equally well on the high seas or in shallow rivers.

Shield to protect oarsmen

Hull carved from one large oak tree

Lookout post is called the crow's nest ...

Different-shaped sails make the ship fast and easy to steer

1500s
Sailing ships
Explorers from Europe used fast sailing ships called caravels to explore new lands. With lots of sails, the boats were powered only by wind and the sea currents.

1950s
Hovercraft
The hovercraft skims across the water's surface on a big cushion filled with air. It can also travel over other surfaces, including ice and sand.

Navigation and communications antennae

Inflatable cushion called a skirt

2010s
Colossal cruisers
Modern cruise ships can carry thousands of vacationers at a time. These huge ships have onboard parks, restaurants, and even ice-skating rinks!

Back of a ship is the stern

Multistory decks ...

Plain sailing
This sailboat is built sideways.
Only the mast stands upright, built onto
a 1x1 round plate with bar and hole.

1x1 round plate with bar and hole

Build it!

Travelers steered and moved the rafts with a wooden oar

I'M DIVING INTO HISTORY!

Reed held the logs together

3100s BCE
Egyptian sailboats
The Ancient Egyptians were the first people to use sails on their vessels. The sails caught the wind, allowing boats to travel faster along the slow-flowing River Nile.

Broad cloth sail

Around 5000 BCE
Log rafts
The first rafts were built in Southeast Asia. They were made from logs and tied together with reeds. Explorers used these craft to travel as far as Australia!

Lookout position

Rudder for steering

1840s
Steam-powered ships
Steam-powered iron ships transformed the world of shipping. These powerful vessels could travel quickly, making journeys in about half the time of a sailing ship.

Oar

1620s
Early submersibles
The first-ever underwater craft was built in England and launched in the River Thames. It was powered by 12 oarsmen and made from wood and oiled leather.

Foldable mast

Funnel

Build it!

The right shape
The main sub build is only one stud wide, but 1x3 plates on both sides give it a rounder shape.

1x3 plate

Joystick

27

Down on the farm

Many farmers rely on specialized machines to help them grow plants and raise animals. Modern farm vehicles combine power and technology to perform jobs with maximum speed and efficiency.

Record breakers

The Big Bud 747 is claimed to be the **world's biggest tractor**. It has eight enormous tires and weighs 30 times more than a family car.

American blacksmith John Deere invented the first-ever steel plow in 1837. It could **handle even the toughest soil**, making life much easier for farmers.

Combine harvester ▼

This mighty machine combines lots of harvesting jobs in one. It cuts crops, then separates them into grain and straw. The straw is ejected at the back, ready to be made into hay bales.

Grain storage tank

Grain unloading pipe

Front attachment is called the header

Cutter bar cuts the crop

Surrounding windows for maximum visibility

Hood protects the engine

Build it!

Pin it!

The back wheels of the tractor connect to LEGO® Technic connector pegs. The front wheels click onto smaller wheel connectors.

LEGO Technic connector peg

2x2 plate with wheel connectors

▲ Tractor

Every farm needs a tractor. This heavyweight helper can do all kinds of tasks, from lifting loads to plowing fields or pulling trailers.

Huge, chunky wheels don't slip in the mud

Seed-planting plane ▶

Planting large areas with crops, such as wheat, beans, rye, and corn, is fast work with a plane. Seed-planting planes drop seeds over a wide area. This process is called aerial seeding.

"HAY"— IT'S A PLANE!

Small cockpit for pilot

Seeds stored in a hold

Seeds released below the fuselage

Propeller

Hay bales

Insulated tank keeps the milk cool

Access hatch for checking the load

Hose attaches to rear to fill tank

Build it!

Drum kit
The tanker drum connects to a brick with a hole and rests in a channel made from a dozen 1x1 slopes.

2x2 dome

1x2 brick with hole

Two rows of 1x1 slopes

▲ Milk tanker

A milk tanker carries milk from a dairy farm to a factory. Its steel container holds up to 6,600 gallons (30,000 liters) of milk—enough to fill about 200 bathtubs.

Back in time

Before tractors, **horses pulled heavy plows** across fields to turn the soil and get it ready for planting.

The farmer held stilts to **steer the plow** and control the depth of the furrows, which were rows of cuts in the soil.

Harness connects to plow

Stilts

Moldboard pushes the soil to one side

Plowshare cuts into the soil

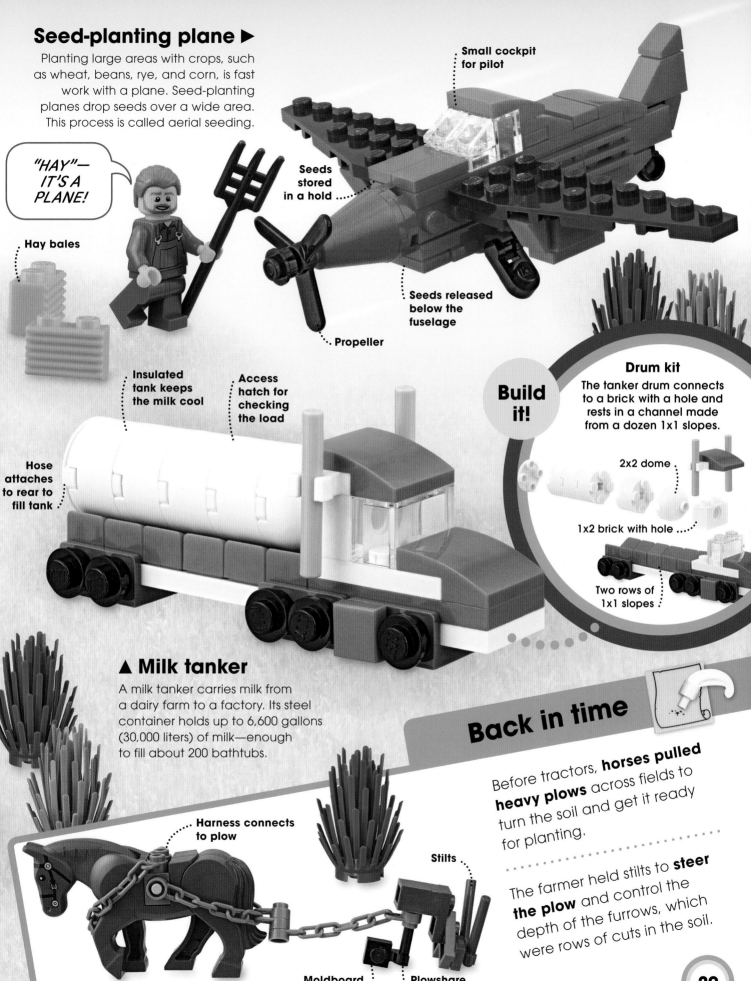

Built for fun

Many vehicles are useful with special jobs to do, but some are made just for people to have a great time. Fast or slow, there are tons of fun vehicles out there to enjoy!

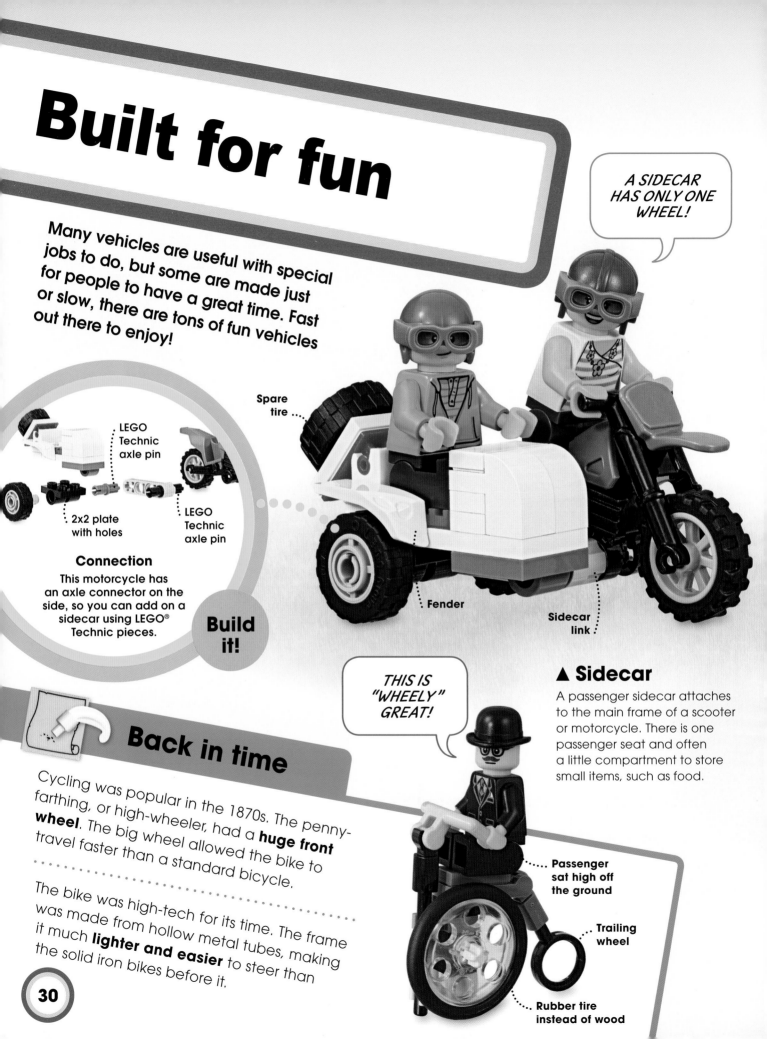

A SIDECAR HAS ONLY ONE WHEEL!

LEGO Technic axle pin

2x2 plate with holes

LEGO Technic axle pin

Connection
This motorcycle has an axle connector on the side, so you can add on a sidecar using LEGO® Technic pieces.

Build it!

Spare tire

Fender

Sidecar link

THIS IS "WHEELY" GREAT!

Back in time

Cycling was popular in the 1870s. The penny-farthing, or high-wheeler, had a **huge front wheel**. The big wheel allowed the bike to travel faster than a standard bicycle.

The bike was high-tech for its time. The frame was made from hollow metal tubes, making it much **lighter and easier** to steer than the solid iron bikes before it.

▲ Sidecar
A passenger sidecar attaches to the main frame of a scooter or motorcycle. There is one passenger seat and often a little compartment to store small items, such as food.

Passenger sat high off the ground

Trailing wheel

Rubber tire instead of wood

30

Space for golf clubs

I'M HAVING A BALL!

Steering wheel

In 2005 in Florida, 3,321 golf carts took part in the **longest-ever golf cart parade**. It took nearly four hours for all the carts to roll past the counting point.

In 2002, Alvaro de Marichalar became the first person to **ride a personal watercraft** across the Atlantic Ocean. He rode 12 hours every day for four months.

Batteries are under the seat

▲ Golf cart

Golf carts carry golfers and their equipment from hole to hole. The carts are built low to the ground to help them stay upright on bumpy terrain. Most are powered by rechargeable batteries.

Jet thruster

Cooler

Steering yoke

Personal watercraft ▶

A thruster at the back of this vehicle sucks in water, then squirts it out with force. This pushes the watercraft forward.

Bumper

THERE'S NO ENGINE ON A KAYAK—JUST ME AND MY PADDLE!

◀ Kayak

Kayaking is a fun way to glide through water. The kayaker uses a paddle with a blade at each end to steer the narrow boat.

Kayaker's seat is called the cockpit

Bow and narrow

The kayak's bowline is a string with studs. It loops around the tiles that make the slender sides.

Build it!

String with two studs

1x6 tile

1x1 brick with side stud

Most kayaks are made of plastic

Bowline for docking

Up in the air

People have devised many different ways of getting vehicles to fly. The first-ever airplane flight lasted only three seconds. Today, some aircraft can fly for thousands of miles without stopping to refuel.

NEEOW!

Record breakers

The **largest blimp** ever built was *Graf Zeppelin II*. The blimp, built in the 1930s, was three times longer than a jumbo jet.

The **tiniest unmanned aerial vehicle** is smaller than a quarter. It was designed to carry out search-and-rescue missions.

Spreader bar

Propeller

Float

▲ Seaplane
Instead of wheels, the seaplane has two floats so it can take off from and land on water. They are mostly used in areas with few airfields.

Lightweight frame

Spinning blades keep the drone in the air

Remote control

Drone ▲
An unmanned aerial vehicle (UAV), or drone, is a flying machine that's operated by remote control. Drones carry special equipment to film the land below or monitor weather. Some even deliver packages!

Build it!

Jumper plate to center wings

Transparent small radar dish piece

In a spin
A clear dish piece on the front of the seaplane creates the illusion of a propeller spinning so fast it is almost invisible.

Ducted fan
for steering

Helium-filled
balloon

Rear propeller
moves the ship
through the air

▲ Blimp

The blimp is filled with a gas
called helium that's lighter
than air, making the ship float.
Propellers move it forward
and keep it on course.

Passenger
cabin

Build it!

Horse power

The wings and tail of
this old-fashioned plane
are connected by two
LEGO® pieces more often
used to make horse carts.

Horse cart
harness

Telescope
pieces

Flame-resistant
material

Hot air balloon ▶

A gas burner under the
balloon heats the air inside it.
As the air gets hotter, the
balloon rises. To travel back
down, the pilot pulls a cord to
let air out of the balloon.

Basket for the pilot
and passengers

Bottom of envelope
is called the skirt

Back in time

More than 100 years ago, the first
powered planes took to the skies.
The double sets of wings provided lifting
power and made the plane easy to steer.

To fly the plane, the pilot lay flat on
his stomach on top of the lower wing.
He moved a small set of wings at the
front to make the plane go up or down.

Wings were
made of wood
and cloth

Rear

Front

Thin struts
connected the wings

At the airport

There are many vehicles at an airport besides airplanes. Each airport vehicle has a special task to do and is designed to make sure that every plane is ready to take off or land.

Record breakers

Jumbo jets have a wingspan of 250 ft (76.2 m). That means **eight double-decker buses** could line up from wing to wing! The **world's largest fuel tanker** is made for airports. It holds 15,000 gallons (68,000 liters) of fuel—almost twice as much as normal road fuel tankers.

Build it!

Pose your hose
The fuel truck's rigid hose is made from two L-shaped bars. They are connected by a tube holder with clip.

L-shaped bar

Tube holder with clip

1x2 plate with top clip

2x2 turntable

Hose delivers fuel to the plane

Fuel gauge

Filter

▲ Aircraft refueler

Airplanes need fuel before they can take off. The fuel truck has a hose to connect it to an underground jet fuel store. The truck delivers the fuel to a plane's tanks.

THESE CARS CAN CARRY HUNDREDS OF BAGS AT ONCE.

Covers protect baggage in bad weather

Car

Tug

▲ Baggage car

Luggage is loaded onto baggage cars. The cars are linked together and pulled to the plane by a tug vehicle. Each car has an automatic parking brake for extra safety.

Top deck

Planes often have to park a long way from the passenger terminal. The shuttle bus transfers passengers safely to and from the aircraft. Inside, there is space for passengers and their carry-on luggage.

Elevator

▲ Jumbo jet

This flying giant is designed for long-distance passenger flights. Double-decker "superjumbo" jets like this one have room for more than 850 people in their cabins.

Four engines power the plane

Driver-controlled safety doors

Passenger seating

Rear panel

Refrigerated food crate

◀ Catering truck

Airline meals are prepared on the ground and delivered to the aircraft. The truck's body can be raised up to the door of the plane so that the crew can unload the food easily.

Ramp to the plane door

Hydraulic lift raises and lowers the container

Up and down

The ramp to the plane door can be raised and lowered using two 1x2 hinge bricks.

1x2 grille

1x4 white brick

1x2 hinge brick

Build it!

Flying through time

For hundreds of years, people looked up at the birds and wished they could fly, too. Eventually, inventors found clever ways to get airborne. Today, flying is part of everyday life for millions of people.

Balloon, called an envelope, made of silk

Passenger area

1780s
Hot air balloons
The first hot air balloons were developed in France. They allowed people to take to the sky for the first time ever.

... Stabilizer helped control the plane

1910s
Monoplanes
Around 1910, engineers developed single-wing planes called monoplanes. The machines were faster and sturdier than earlier double-winged planes and could travel longer distances.

Wheels for take-off and landing

Tail rotor steered helicopter

Rotor

1930s
Helicopters
Ideas for an aircraft that could lift straight into the air were first drawn up about 500 years ago. In the 1930s, the first helicopters took to the air with spinning blades called a rotor. Rotors let helicopters take off and land vertically.

Some designs had no closing doors

2010s
Drones
Flying drones, also called unmanned aerial vehicles, are piloted from the ground. This means the machines can travel to places that manned vehicles cannot, such as close to active volcanoes.

Camera can film the ground below

Lightweight frame

2x2 round plate with hooks

Small radar dish

Build it!

Make a drone of your own
Not all drones have four propellers. So even if you don't have a plate with four hooks, you can still build a realistic drone.

1x1 plate with clip

1x2 plate with clip

Build it!

Bird-shaped cloth wing

1850s
Gliders
Early glider engineers studied birds to learn how they stayed in the air. The machines they developed had angled wings, called airfoils, which caught more air than flat wings.

Wooden frame

1900s
Engine-powered airplanes
The earliest engine-powered planes had basic engines and could travel short distances easily. Their designs were inspired by successful gliders.

Rear rudder turned the plane

Elevators made the plane go up or down

1950s
Passenger jets
The development of the jet engine meant that airplanes could fly faster and farther than ever before. Air travel became a common way for lots of people to travel long distances.

Main body called a fuselage

Jet engine sits under the wing

2010s
Personal flyers
Most personal flyers, or jet packs, available today are powered by gas engines. These compact vehicles are designed to transport a solo pilot over a short distance.

Thrusters provide power to get airborne

Hand control

TAKE-OFF WAS EASY—NOW HOW DO I LAND THIS THING?

In the snow

Snow vehicles are tough and made to move through the worst wintry conditions. They can travel through snow, ice, strong winds, numbing cold, and swirling blizzards.

Record breakers

The Iditarod is the **longest dog-sled race** in the world. Teams of 16 huskies and a driver race 1,049 miles (1,688 km) over the frozen ground of Alaska.

In 1977, the Russian icebreaker *Arktika* became the **first surface ship** to reach the North Pole.

GETTING AROUND IN THIS WEATHER IS "SNOW" JOKE!

Handlebars for steering ....

Ski runner

... Continuous track grips the ice and snow

Snowmobile ▲

The snowmobile has a powerful engine, continuous tracks, and ski runners that curve upward. The runners stop the vehicle from plowing into the snow.

... Very high-frequency antenna

Crane at front and rear for lifting gear onto the ship

▲ Icebreaker ship

When it's so cold that even the sea freezes, the icebreaker clears a path for other ships. Its shape and extra-strong construction means it can power through ice that's 9 ft (2.8 m) deep—that's a bit deeper than an Olympic-size swimming pool!

Double hull gives the boat two watertight layers :

Pointed bow crushes ice

Arctic articulation

A notched string with end studs links the sled to the dogs. Each dog wears a small bracket piece connected to a sideways 1x1 plate with a top clip.

Minifigure neck bracket

Notched string with end studs

Build it!

TO GET A DOG SLED TEAM TO GO, SAY "MUSH!"

Sled bag carries cargo

The driver stands on foot boards

Tugline

Husky sled ▲

In the Arctic, teams of hardworking husky dogs pull heavy loads in sleds. The sleds have skilike runners designed to glide easily over ice and snow.

Powerful light for plowing in limited visibility

▶ Snow plow

Even after a heavy snowstorm, the massive might of the snow plow soon clears the way. Its huge blade pushes snow and ice off the road.

Snow tires so the plow doesn't get stuck

Curved blade pushes snow to the side

Back in time

Driver and passenger seating

Curved shield

Reins

Horse-drawn sleighs were built for speed, with lightweight bodies and slim runners for gliding over packed snow. Sleighs were used to carry passengers and deliver the mail.

Passengers sat behind a **curved shield** to protect them from spray kicked up by the horses.

Runner glides over snow

Over rough terrain

When the going gets tough, these machines really get going! Some vehicles are designed or modified to handle all kinds of challenging off-road terrain, from sands to swamplands.

Roof protects passengers from the hot sun

Grille allows air to enter so engine doesn't overheat

All-terrain tire

SEE YA LATER, ALLIGATOR!

▲ Safari truck

An off-road safari truck has rugged tires and four-wheel drive to cope with desert dunes, flash floods, and rocky river beds. The body is long, flat, and open for wildlife-spotting.

Steering

The skimmer's two propellers slot onto a nozzle piece. A claw fits onto the nozzle handle to make a steering lever.

Nozzle

Claw piece

Propeller

1x2 jumper plate

Propeller

▼ Airboat

This boat is perfect for skimming through shallow water, such as swamps. Instead of an underwater engine, it is powered by a big fan, which pushes the boat forward.

Build it!

Boat made of lightweight material, such as aluminum

Driver controls the boat from the back seat

Flat bottom for shallow water

Nozzle piece .... Tube holder with clip

Unlocking the cage

Nozzle pieces and tube holders with clips combine to make the protective roll cage of this dune buggy.

Build it!

Support frame made from steel tubes

Engine at the rear

Body made of fiberglass

▲ Dune buggy

Many vehicles struggle to drive over sand. Dune buggies have a simple design with a lightweight body and wide, soft tires to help them grip the sand.

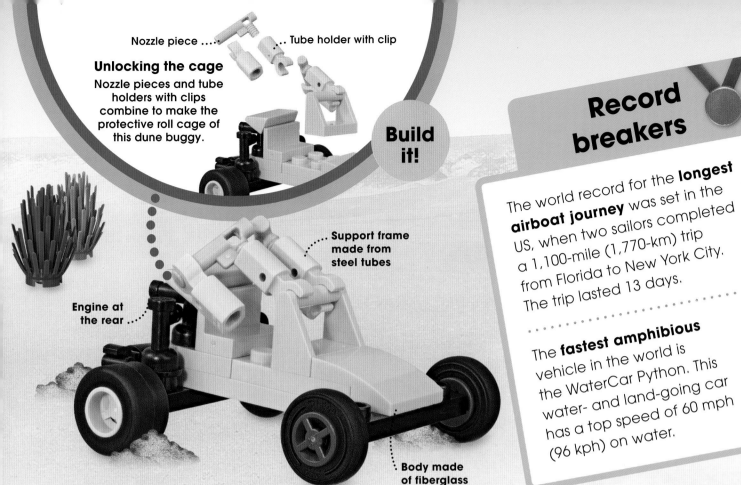

Record breakers

The world record for the **longest airboat journey** was set in the US, when two sailors completed a 1,100-mile (1,770-km) trip from Florida to New York City. The trip lasted 13 days.

The **fastest amphibious** vehicle in the world is the WaterCar Python. This water- and land-going car has a top speed of 60 mph (96 kph) on water.

Radio antenna

◄ Amphibious bus

On the road, this sightseeing vehicle is an ordinary tourist bus. However, the vehicle's watertight body lets it slip into the water for a river cruise, too!

Captain operates the vehicle from the cab

Watertight hull

Tires can be deflated from the cab for driving over sand

Goods on the go

On land, over water, and in the air, vehicles transport goods from place to place. They carry big and small loads of everything imaginable, from electronics to food—and even this book!

Extra-large hold can carry vehicles or even other aircraft

Cargo door

Jet engine

Cargo plane ▲

Inside a cargo plane is a huge storage space called the hold. On some planes, the nose or tail opens so that goods can be loaded and stored in the hold.

Horn

Driver's cab

Pilot keeps tracks clear of debris

Diesel engine

Box car

Loading door

Hold for freight

▲ Freight train

Powerful diesel engines pull goods over long distances. Some trains use more than one engine. Freight trains can be made up of nine engines and more than 300 freight cars!

Logging truck ◄

This truck carries large loads of cut-down trees. The truck transports the logs to a sawmill, where special machines cut them into planks.

Hydraulic crane

Claw places logs on the truck's bed

Build it!

Tube with bar

1x2 plate with clip

T-bar

1x2 plate with two bars

Robot arm

Claw piece

Strong lifting arm

All kinds of different bars and clips combine to make the logging truck's crane arm.

Supports stop the logs from rolling off

One container can hold 6,000 shoe boxes

Bridge is positioned high up to see over the stacks of containers

Container ship ▶

Stacked high with massive metal boxes, container ships move freight over water. Each container is the same size and shape. This means they can be stacked like building blocks to make use of as much space as possible.

Containers fill the hull below deck

I HOPE THAT BOX CAR IS FULL OF COFFEE.

Fuel tanker

Record breakers

The **world's largest container ship** can carry 21,413 containers. At 1,312 ft (400 m) long, five jumbo jets can line up on its deck.

The **largest cargo plane** is the Antonov An-225. It was designed to carry a space shuttle and has 32 wheels on its landing gear.

Trailer

Tractor unit

Four rear wheels support the heavy trailer

▲ Semi-truck

A semi-truck hauls goods on the road. Freight is packed in the long trailer behind the tractor unit, which contains the engine and the driver's cab.

The truck bends at this joint so it can steer around corners

On the rails

Traveling on rail tracks is a quick way to move people and goods from place to place. At first, trains were pulled by horses. Later, they were powered by steam. Today's trains use diesel and electricity to speed across the land.

1x4 click hinge brick

1x2 click hinge brick

1x2 click hinge plate

It all clicks
Use click hinges to make a strong crane that will only move when you want it to.

Build it!

Cabin can turn in a full circle

Crane boom

Wheels are designed for railroad tracks

▲ Tie crane
When it's time to lay new track or repair an old one, the trusty tie crane swings into action. Its powerful lifting arm has an adjustable claw to lift and set down railroad ties.

Record breakers

The world record for a **high-speed train** running on wheels is 357.2 mph (574.8 kph). That's almost twice as fast as a Formula 1® race car!

The GER handcar holds the world record for the **longest distance traveled** by handcar. In 1997, the handcar traveled over 126 miles (202 km) of track in 12 hours.

WHOOSH!

▲ High-speed train
High-speed trains reach their top speed on straight tracks, where they don't have to slow down for bends. The trains are powered by electricity.

Wheels are replaced frequently because they wear out quickly at high speeds

The nose is angled for a streamlined shape

Normal road vehicle body

◄ Road-rail vehicle

These versatile vehicles have two sets of wheels. They can be driven both on the road and along railroad lines. Road-rail vehicles transport track inspectors and repair crews.

Rubber tires for road driving

Grooved metal wheels are lowered onto train tracks when needed

On the right track

The switcher is built with eight train wheels attached to four 2x2 plates with wheel connectors—much narrower than most LEGO® trains.

2x2 plate with wheel connectors

Train wheel

Build it!

Diesel engine

Buffer beam

Buffers for pushing carriages

▲ Switcher

The switcher is a small, powerful engine that pushes other trains. At a station or rail yard, it moves carriages to where they need to be.

SWITCHERS ARE SLOW BUT STRONG.

Back in time

Before road-rail vehicles, railroad workers used **handcars** to travel along tracks. They took turns pushing and pulling a seesawlike bar to move the car forward.

The car held up to **six workers**. One man pushed the car to get it started, then jumped on as four others worked the bar to gain speed. The car went at about 8 mph (12 kph)—the same speed as a fast human jogger.

The bar attached to a crank, which moved the wheels

Platform for workers to stand on

Chugging through time

All aboard for a journey through the story of railroads! From horse-drawn coal carts to super-powered, high-tech passenger trains, vehicles on the rails have become faster and faster over time.

Many mine carts were used to carry loads of coal

1600s
Mine carts
The first railroads were designed to carry heavy loads away from mines in small carts. The carts were slim so that they could easily fit inside narrow mineshafts.

Hopper

Hand rail for standing riders

1870s
Cable cars
Cable cars were invented in California. The cars attached to cables under the street, which were wound in by a steam-powered engine. This moved the cars.

Passenger seat

Driver's cab

Chimney let out steam and smoke

1920s
Steam locomotives
In the 1920s, steam-powered trains had become the fastest, most popular way to travel. Sleek express trains were designed to carry passengers nonstop over long distances.

Future
Vacuum-tube trains
The future of train travel might be vacuum-tube trains. These trains travel at high speeds through specially built tubes and are powered by magnets!

Tube

Each cabin may fit up to eight passengers

1x4 tile

1x1 plate with top clip

2x2x2 dustbin

Radar dish

Vacuum packed
With its smooth tiled top, the vacuum-tube train fits snugly in the sideways dustbin.

Barreling along

This barrel-shaped engine is built sideways—except for its funnel, which is built upside down.

1x2 plate with ring above

2x2 round plates as steam

1x1 cone

Barrel

Build it!

TICKETS, PLEASE!

Gear powered by steam

Boiler

1800s
Steam-powered engines
Early steam-powered train engines were lighter, more reliable, and much faster than any other engine at the time.

First-class coaches had roofs; others were open-topped

1860s
Subway trains
The first underground railroad was built in London, England. Small, powerful steam engines pulled gas-lit passenger carriages through specially built tunnels.

Coupler connected to other carriages

Front carriage was called the power car

Sloped, streamlined nose

1960s
High-speed trains
The bodies of these trains were streamlined—designed to stop air from slowing it down. They ran on special tracks and were powered by electricity picked up from overhead lines.

1980s
Driverless trains
Trains operated by a central computer system, instead of a driver, first carried commuters and tourists in the 1980s. The computer controlled the trains' speed, making sure that they ran on time.

Passenger window

Passengers could sit in the front of some computer-operated trains since there was no driver onboard

Build it!

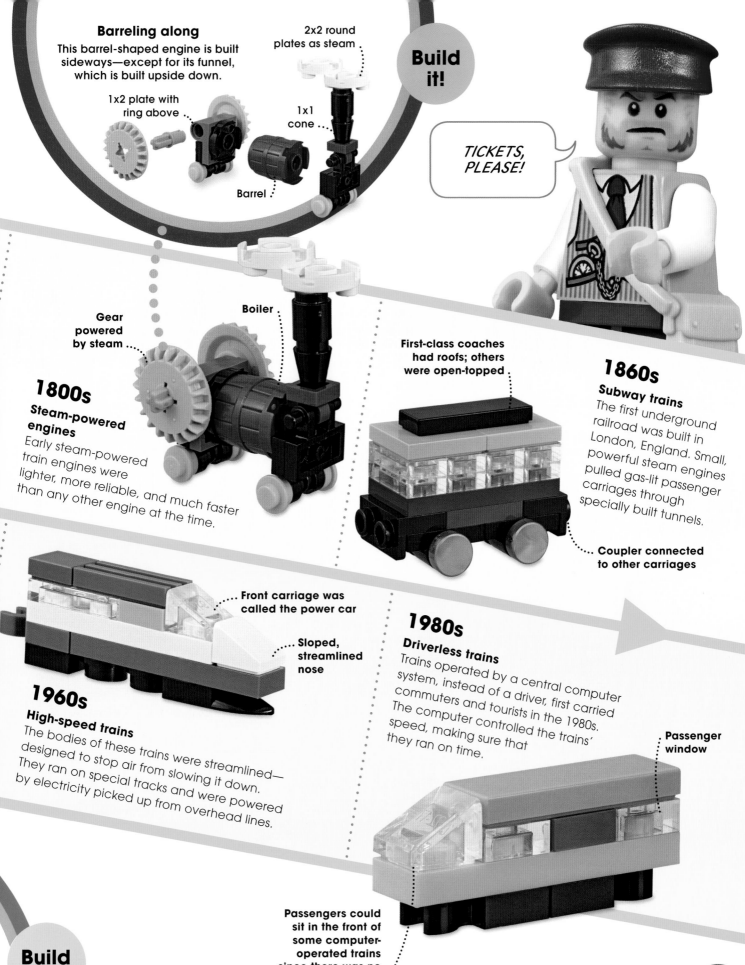

On the move

People rely on vehicles to get to work, school, and stores; to go on vacation; or to visit their friends. When people travel together in one large vehicle, it cuts down on air pollution—and means fewer traffic jams, too.

Flashing stop light

Side-view mirror helps the driver see children and other traffic

"Stop" arm tells traffic to halt

Back in time

About 150 years ago in Tokyo, Japan, the **first rickshaws appeared**. These small two-wheeled carts had handles so they could be pulled by a person.

Rickshaws became popular in many Asian cities. Pulling the cart was hard work. **Bicycle versions** were invented about 30 years later. Many rickshaw drivers preferred pedal power.

School bus ▲

The school bus is a safe way for children to get to and from school. In many countries, they are bright yellow, making them easy to spot from a distance. Flashing lights warn other drivers when children are getting on and off.

Sun canopy shaded passenger

Handles made from wood

To the side

The curved sides of the ferry are built sideways onto angle plates. The railings are sideways plates with bars.

Row of 1x2 angle plates ...

1x2 plate with bar ....

Build it!

◀ Ferry

Ferries shuttle back and forth across a stretch of water. Trucks and passenger cars drive onto the boat using a ramp. The vehicles are parked on deck while the passengers ride on the passenger deck.

Bridge

Ramp for cars and trucks

Passenger car

▼ Minivan

There's room in here for the whole family, plus luggage, bikes, and surfboards—even the family pet! Many minivans include roof racks on top to hold even more of the family's baggage.

Roof rack increases luggage space ....

Back door opens for easy loading

Record breakers

The world's **shortest ferry ride** is in Toronto, Canada. It takes just 90 seconds to cross from the mainland to the city's island airport.

On South Bass Island in Ohio, the school bus is actually a plane! Students take a **four-minute flight** to school on the mainland.

Walls can slide out to make more space

Air conditioner

Motorhome/RV ▶

These buslike vehicles are like mini homes on wheels, with all the facilities needed for extended road trips. Cleverly designed to pack facilities into a small space, some luxury models even have a home theater!

Inner door section

2x3 plate connects the two door sections

Open up

The sliding door of the motorhome is held snugly in place between the roof and a smooth tile floor.

Build it!

Large interior has a sleeping area, kitchen, and bathroom

Out west

The "Wild West" is seriously big, and vehicles are essential there to help people get around. From coaches of the past to today's versatile trucks, vehicles have always been important to residents in the west.

Driver and passenger cabin

Bed for hauling cargo

Tailgate opens outward

▶ Pickup truck

A pickup truck transports everything from farm equipment to animal feed. Its open carrying area, called a bed, has sides and a hinged flap called a tailgate that opens for easy loading.

All-terrain tires

GOOD THING THIS TRUCK HAS A BED. I'M "TIRED"!

Back in time

The **horse-drawn stagecoach** was a popular way to travel in the "Old West." The carriages carried passengers, goods, or mail.

There were very few roads, so stagecoaches were built to withstand **rough terrain**, with strong wheels. The driver sat high at the front, keeping a lookout for hazards ahead.

Luggage rack

Driver's seat

Passenger cabin

Ventilation holes

Build it!

One good turn
Use a turntable with tiles around it to make an articulated transporter that can turn smoothly.

... 2x2 turntable

▲ Animal transporter
These special trucks move livestock, such as cattle. Compartments inside the trailer keep the animals safe and calm, with lots of fresh air. A ramp helps them to get on and off easily.

Extra coal is carried in a cart called the tender

The funnel lets air in so the fire burns better ....

Steam dome

Main rod

Steam train ▲
Steam trains arrived in the 1860s and moved passengers and goods quickly across the land. Modern trains replaced steam trains in daily life, but there are many steam trains that still take passengers on exciting rides just for fun!

Record breakers

In 1869, the US Transcontinental Railroad was completed. **Steam locomotives** reduced the journey time from New York to California from a few months to one week.

The **most luxurious stagecoach** was the Concord. Its suspension made for a comfortable ride even on bumpy roads.

51

To the extreme

DON'T TRY THIS AT HOME!

Some vehicles push the limits of what a mobile machine can do. Special engines and features help them to perform impressive stunts that leave ordinary vehicles in the dust.

Record breakers

The fastest **superbikes can reach** a speed of 60 mph (96 kph) in just three seconds!

The **biggest monster trucks** have wheels so large that a human adult can stand up inside the rim.

Tough plastic windshield helps air flow over the rider

Streamlined body

Superbike ▲

This two-wheeled machine is designed for power and speed. A superbike weighs about six times less than a family car but is nearly twice as powerful.

Pickup truck or SUV body

▶ Monster truck

Monster trucks are pickup trucks or sport utility vehicles (SUVs) with souped-up engines and super-springy suspensions. These cool creations race and perform stunts at big shows.

Soft tires roll over large obstacles, such as cars

Many trucks have features, such as fangs, to make them look like animals

Front shock absorber

52

Springing surprises

Look closely and you'll see silver 1x1 round plates behind the ATV's wheels, representing its shock absorbers.

3x4 mudguard with plate

Stack of 1x1 round plates

Build it!

Radio antenna

READY TO ROLL?

Handlebars instead of a steering wheel

▶ All-terrain vehicle (ATV)

An ATV's wide tires can handle all kinds of off-road surfaces. The body is mounted on coiled springs called shock absorbers, so it can bounce over even the rockiest trails.

Low tire pressure helps ATVs travel over snow, mud, and loose sand

SOME POWERBOATS HAVE CLOSED COCKPITS.

Build it!

4x6 curved angled slope

Slide plate

Rugged rides

Use smooth-bottomed slide plates on the underside of your boats to glide them effortlessly over carpet lakes and oceans!

Powerful engine

Extra-long body

▲ Powerboat

These watercraft are made to slice through the water at fast speeds. A powerboat's sleek shape and lightweight materials help it to move quickly.

Hull is filled with plastic foam for a gentler ride over rough water

Out of this world

Spacecraft help people to explore the universe beyond Earth. Each space vehicle is designed to do a special job and is built out of materials that will not break in the harsh conditions of space.

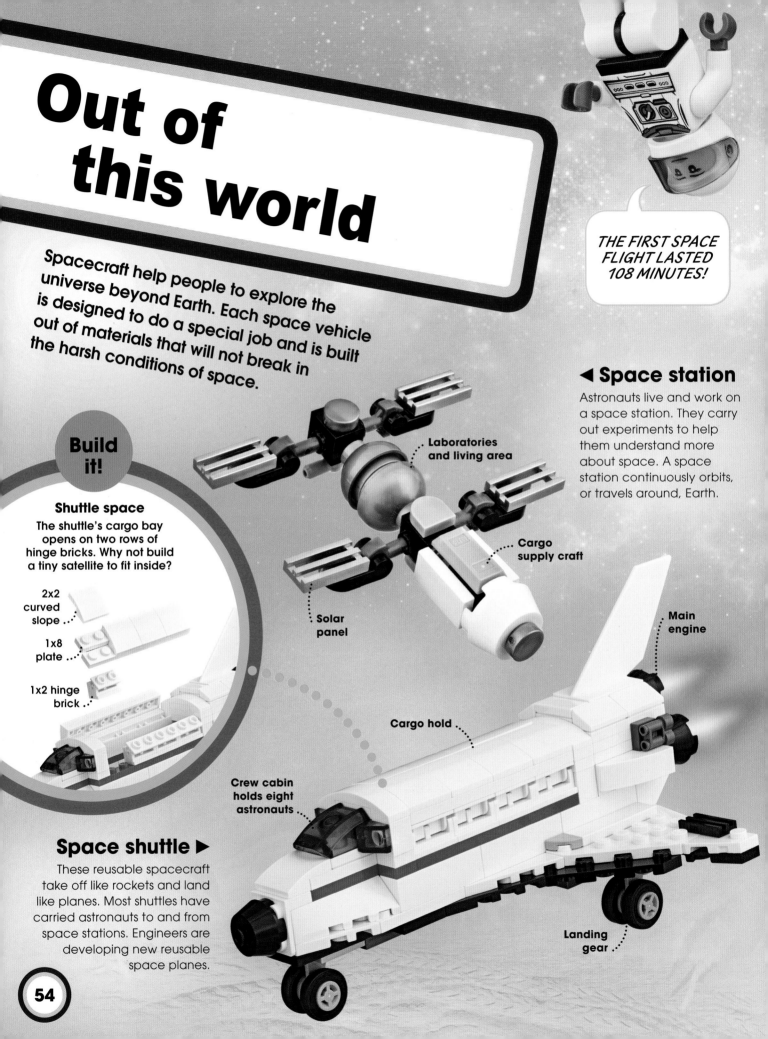

THE FIRST SPACE FLIGHT LASTED 108 MINUTES!

Build it!

Shuttle space
The shuttle's cargo bay opens on two rows of hinge bricks. Why not build a tiny satellite to fit inside?

2x2 curved slope ...

1x8 plate ...

1x2 hinge brick ...

◀ Space station
Astronauts live and work on a space station. They carry out experiments to help them understand more about space. A space station continuously orbits, or travels around, Earth.

Laboratories and living area

Cargo supply craft

Solar panel

Main engine

Cargo hold

Crew cabin holds eight astronauts ...

Space shuttle ▶
These reusable spacecraft take off like rockets and land like planes. Most shuttles have carried astronauts to and from space stations. Engineers are developing new reusable space planes.

Landing gear ...

Rocket ▶

Astronauts travel inside the command module

It takes incredible power to break free of the pull of Earth's gravity to reach space. A rocket burns fuel to produce a jet of gas that pushes it upward with awesome force and speed.

This part of the rocket detaches after launch

WHERE DID I PUT THE KEYS TO THIS THING?

Engine cone

Record breakers

The International Space Station **orbits Earth** 16 times in 24 hours. Astronauts on the International Space Station see 16 sunsets every day.

In 1997, the first vehicle to **explore Mars** was a rover called Sojourner. It had six wheels and was only the size of a microwave oven.

Planet rover ▶

A rover is a mobile space research lab. It roams the surface of a planet, moon, or asteroid, taking photos and collecting samples of rocks or dust. Scientists on Earth use remote controls to move the rover.

360° rotating camera

Antenna sends data back to Earth

Robotic arm collects samples

Tough wheels for bumpy terrain

1x2 plate with tubes

Bar

Rocket engine piece

3x3x2 cone

Solid as a rocket

Bars slot through the stacked sections of the rocket's mighty engines to make an extra-strong connection.

Build it!

Blasting off through time

For thousands of years, humans could only observe space from the ground. But in the 20th century, technology advanced so much that vehicles have now made it to the Moon, Mars, and beyond. Where will they go next?

Satellite made of aluminum

Extendable antennae transmitted signals to Earth

1957
Sputnik 1
The world's first space satellite was Russia's Sputnik 1. It was the size of a beach ball and took around 98 minutes to make one full orbit of Earth.

Entry hatch from service module

1969
Lunar module
On July 20, 1969, Apollo 11's lunar landing module Eagle touched down on the Moon's surface. A few minutes later, American Neil Armstrong became the first human to set foot on the Moon.

Adjustable legs for landing on uneven surface

1977
Voyager 1
This spacecraft was launched to study the solar system. At more than 12 billion miles (20 billion km) away, it is the farthest man-made object from Earth and is now in interstellar space.

Science instrument boom

Thermal blanket protects some parts from extreme temperatures

Future
Passenger space planes
Designs for planes that can fly tourists to space are in the works. The reusable planes aim to take passengers into space and stay for a short while before returning to Earth.

Powerful rocket engine

Heat-resistant material

Handful of bricks
The lunar module is made from just 11 pieces. At its center is a 1x1 brick with four side studs.

1x1 brick with four side studs

1x1 plate with bar

Robot arm

Docking maneuvers

2x2 plate with a ring of bars

2x2x2 round brick

LEGO Technic axle

1x1 round plate with hole

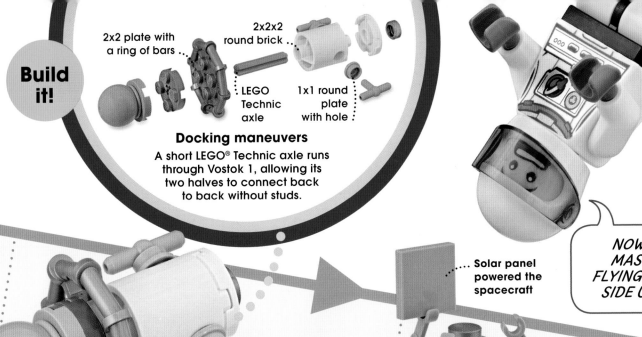

A short LEGO® Technic axle runs through Vostok 1, allowing its two halves to connect back to back without studs.

NOW TO MASTER FLYING RIGHT SIDE UP . . .

.... Solar panel powered the spacecraft

1960s

Vostok 1

Russian Yuri Gagarin was the first person to travel in space. Vostok 1 was controlled remotely from Earth because no one knew if zero-gravity would affect a human's ability to move or think.

Antenna

Descent capsule carried Gagarin back to Earth

Arm collected samples from the surface of the Moon

1966

Surveyor 1

This spacecraft was equipped with cameras to send data and images of the Moon's surface to Earth. It proved that it was possible for spacecraft to land on the Moon and perform tasks.

1980s

Space shuttle

Designed to travel to space and back, the US fleet of five space shuttles flew 135 missions and traveled more than 542 million miles (873 million km) before they were retired in 2011.

Vertical tail

Safety hatch

2000s

Mars Exploration Rover

In 2003, scientists landed two rover vehicles on the planet Mars. Since then, the mobile data collectors have sent thousands of images of Mars back to Earth.

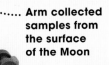

Disk-shaped radio antenna ....

Puncture-proof metal wheel ....

IT'S HARD TO RUN IN THIS SUIT!

Into the future!

Vehicles have really moved ahead over the years. The latest technology has created modes of transportation that can do things that were once unimaginable. Could some of these amazing machines be the vehicles of the future?

THIS SURE BEATS WALKING TO SCHOOL!

◀ Personal flyer

Also known as a jet pack, the personal flyer is powered by two tiny but powerful engines.

Neck bracket

T-bar

String with studs

Holder

Harness

Engine powered by jet fuel

Pack in the details
Build lots of unusual small pieces onto a minifigure neck bracket to make a complex-looking jet pack.

Build it!

GPS antenna

Laser scanner

Video cameras

Pedestrian sensor

Self-driving car ▶

A central computer drives this vehicle. The computer constantly receives information from cameras, GPS navigation units, and sensors to keep it from hitting anything.

Radar

Central computer

▶ Electric flyer

Future aircraft could be powered by electric motors, making them less polluting than fuel-powered craft. This design uses battery-powered propellers to stay airborne.

I'M FLYING INTO THE FUTURE!

Steering mechanism

Mini propeller moves the craft up and forward

Float for landing on water

Record breakers

One **personal flyer** prototype can reach a top speed of 200 mph (320 kph). That's almost as fast as an average race car!

In 2017, Chinese scientists successfully **teleported an object** from Earth into space. The object was a single, incredibly tiny particle called a photon.

Passenger

Digital body scanners

Radio waves

Build it!

Beaming from here to there

The teleportation beams are lightning-bolt pieces that connect to the beam-emitters using claw pieces.

Tap piece

Claw piece

Two small radar dishes

Lightning-bolt piece

◀ Teleporter

Teleportation means transporting something instantly from one place to another. This is possible, in theory. Teleporting a person hasn't been achieved yet, but maybe one day it will be an easy way to travel.

Useful bricks

All LEGO® bricks are useful, but some are more helpful than others when it comes to building vehicles. Don't worry if you don't have all of these parts. Get things going with the pieces you do have.

Brick basics

Bricks are the basis of most LEGO® builds. They come in many shapes and sizes and are named according to size.

2x3 brick overhead view

2x3 brick side view

Plates are the same as bricks, only slimmer. Three stacked plates are the same height as a standard brick.

1x2 plate

3 1x2 plates   **1x2 brick**

Tiles look like plates, but without any studs on top. This gives them a smooth look for more realistic builds.

2x2 tile   **2x2 round tile**

1x6 tile

Slopes are any bricks with diagonal angles. They can be big, small, curved, or inverted (upside down).

1x2 slope   **1x2 inverted slope**

1x3 curved slope

Cool connectors

Jumper plates allow you to "jump" the usual grid of LEGO studs. Use them to center things like micro-scale plane wings and cockpits.

1x2 jumper plate

There are different kinds of **bricks with side studs**. They all allow you to build outward, as well as upward.

1x1 brick with two side studs   **1x2/2x2 angle plate**

Plates with sockets and **plates with balls** link together to make flexible connections for things like trailers and train cars.

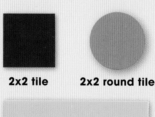

Ball joint socket   **2x2 brick with ball joint**

Any piece with a **bar** can fit onto a piece with a **clip**. Use clips and bars to make moving parts, such as crane arms.

1x2 plate with bar   **1x1 plate with clip**

Hinge plates can give your builds side-to-side movement. **Hinge bricks** are used to tilt things up and down.

Hinge plates   **1x2 hinge brick with 2x2 hinge plate**

LEGO® Technic parts expand the range of functions you can build into your vehicles.

LEGO Technic beam

LEGO Technic friction pin

Wheels

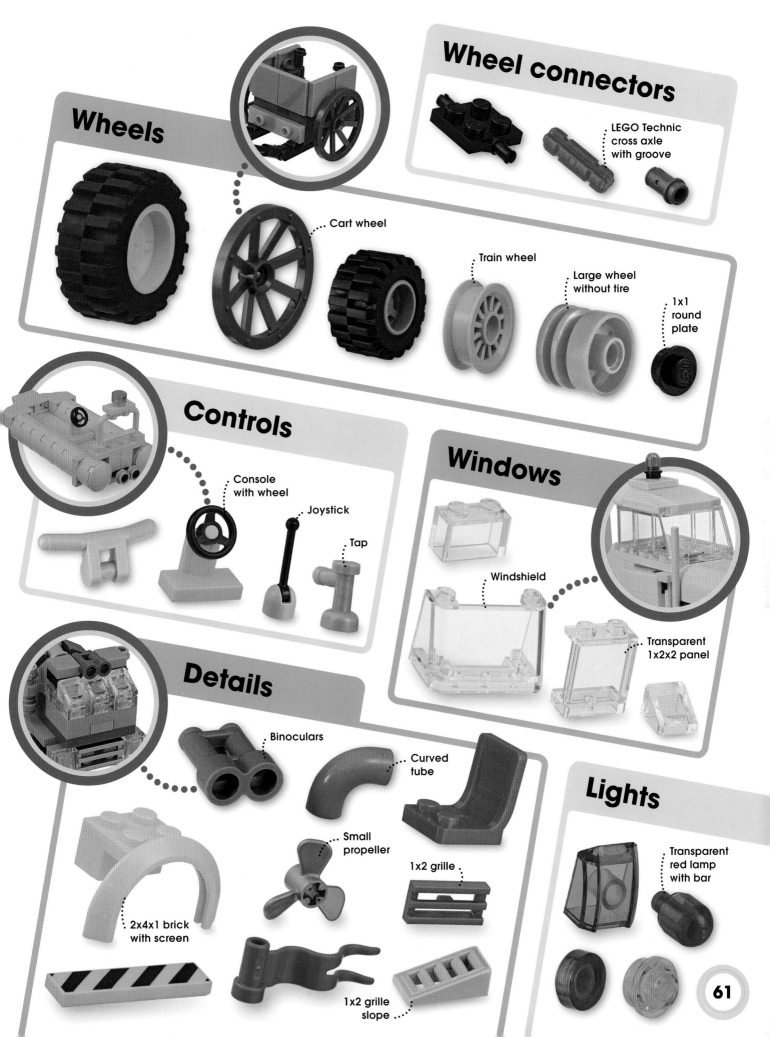

Cart wheel

Train wheel

Large wheel without tire

1x1 round plate

Wheel connectors

LEGO Technic cross axle with groove

Controls

Console with wheel

Joystick

Tap

Windows

Windshield

Transparent 1x2x2 panel

Details

Binoculars

Curved tube

Small propeller

1x2 grille

2x4x1 brick with screen

1x2 grille slope

Lights

Transparent red lamp with bar

61

Build basics

Every build starts with a single piece—even the most complex-looking ones. Whether you want to build a car, a train, a ship, or a spacecraft, begin by thinking about its size and shape before picking the perfect first piece.

1 Start with a base plate. Then add wheels on top of the plate.

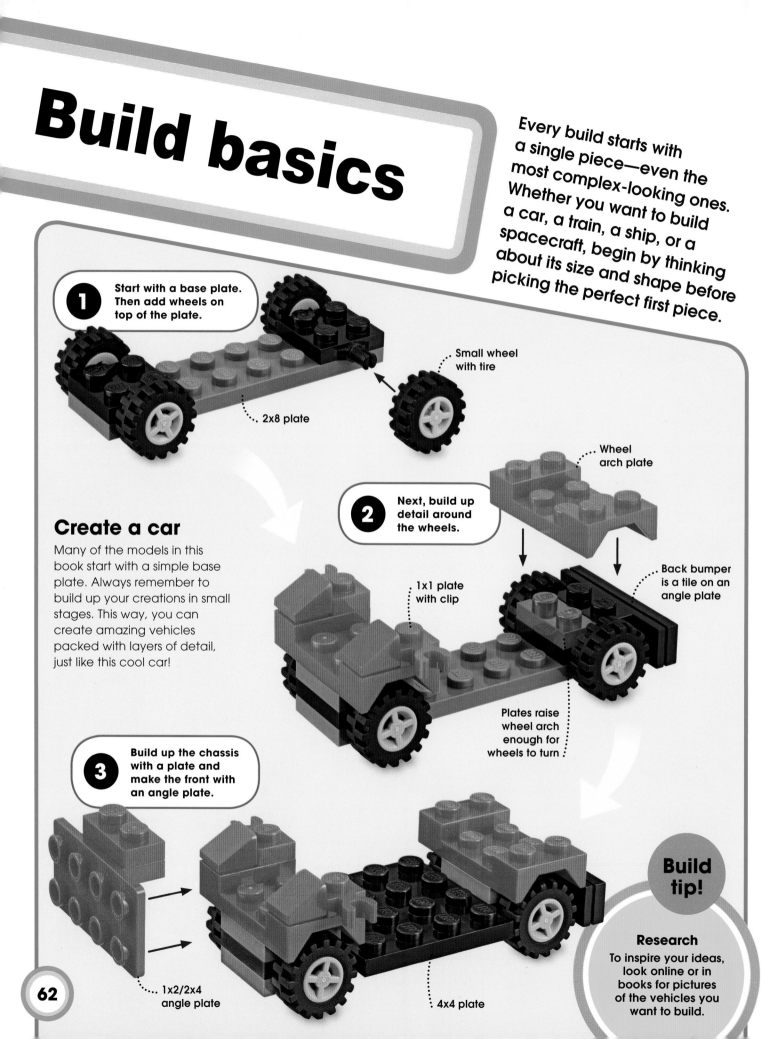

Small wheel with tire

2x8 plate

Wheel arch plate

2 Next, build up detail around the wheels.

Create a car

Many of the models in this book start with a simple base plate. Always remember to build up your creations in small stages. This way, you can create amazing vehicles packed with layers of detail, just like this cool car!

1x1 plate with clip

Back bumper is a tile on an angle plate

Plates raise wheel arch enough for wheels to turn

3 Build up the chassis with a plate and make the front with an angle plate.

1x2/2x4 angle plate

4x4 plate

Build tip!

Research

To inspire your ideas, look online or in books for pictures of the vehicles you want to build.

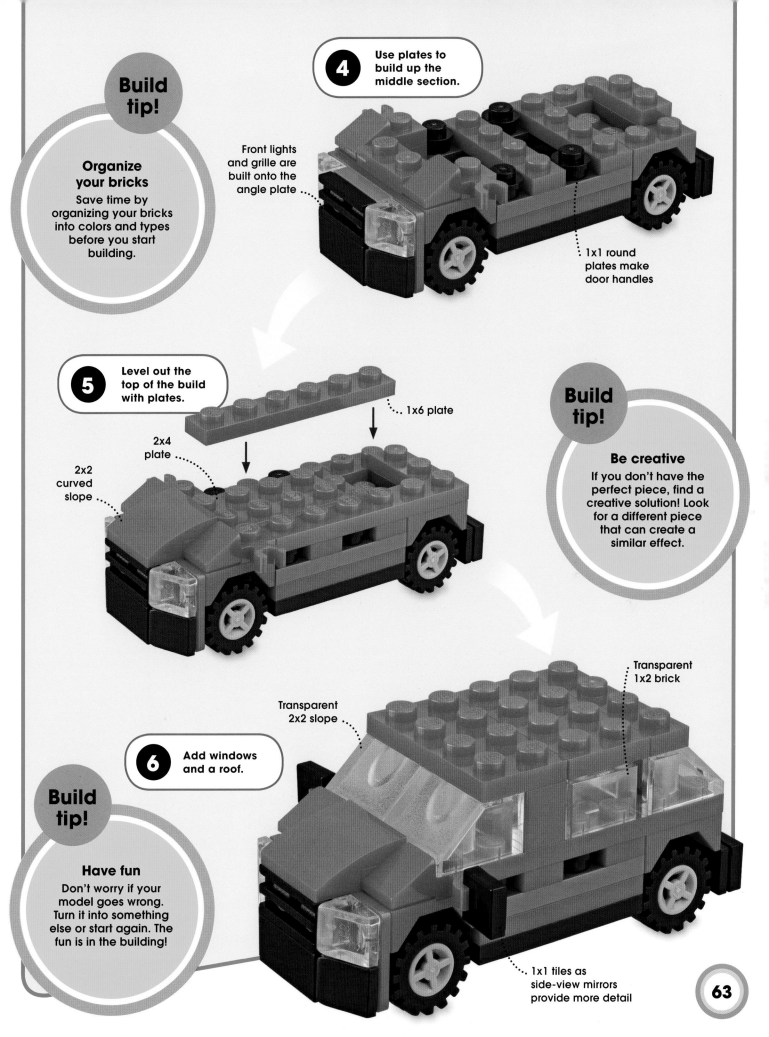

4 Use plates to build up the middle section.

Front lights and grille are built onto the angle plate ......

1x1 round plates make door handles

5 Level out the top of the build with plates.

1x6 plate

2x4 plate

2x2 curved slope

Transparent 1x2 brick

Transparent 2x2 slope

6 Add windows and a roof.

1x1 tiles as side-view mirrors provide more detail

Meet the builders

Jumbo jet
(Barney Main)

The models in this book were created by a talented team of builders who are crazy about LEGO® bricks! We asked them to share some of their secrets . . .

Trading ship
(Simon Pickard)

Fishing trawler
(Jason Briscoe)

Barney Main

How many bricks do you own?
Just about the right amount! But never enough LEGO® Mixel™ eyes.

What is your favorite vehicle?
Hot air balloons are so majestic. They often fly right over our house.

What is the most challenging build you made for this book?
The catering truck has a scissor mechanism so the container can lift up to the plane. It was hard to make the container stay level and not wobble around.

What is your favorite build that you made for this book?
The jumbo jet. It's so sleek and swooshable! And I love the rich, dark blue trim.

What are your top tips for building vehicles?
Get the wheels right! You need big, chunky wheels for a monster truck and small, thin ones for a micro-scale

Catering truck

railroad carriage. Having the right wheels helps the rest of the model take shape. If it's got no wheels, pick another key feature—the propeller, or the wings, or the windshield, or the length of the boat. Then build from the bottom up on a nice big plate.

What is your favorite brick?
1x2 bow. It's really useful on small models for adding strength while keeping the model looking smooth.

If you could build any vehicle in the world, what would it be?
I'd love to build a helicopter from LEGO bricks that could actually fly!

Simon Pickard

How many bricks do you own?
More than two million!

What is your favorite vehicle?
17th-century sailing ships.

What is the most challenging build you made for this book?
The snowmobile. The smaller you get, the more difficult it becomes to build! I was very pleased with the look I still managed to get for this despite the challenging size.

What is your favorite build that you made for this book?
The 19th-century trading ship, because I love history, and the look of this ship at such a small scale really appeals to me.

What are your top tips for building vehicles?
Don't expect to get it right the first time. Sometimes you have to experiment a little to get the right look.

What is your favorite brick?
The 1x1 brick with studs all around, because it enables a wide range of complicated building techniques.

If you could build any vehicle in the world, what would it be?
A space rocket—because who doesn't want to go to space?

Snowmobile

Jason Briscoe

Road roller

How many bricks do you own?
Approximately two to three million—and counting!

What is the most challenging build you made for this book?
Probably the road roller, as I wanted to use the half cylinders and had to work up a design that looked right and made best use of the part.

What is your favorite build that you made for this book?
The fishing trawler. It has some really cool touches, like the red macaroni tubes on the roof.

What are your top tips for building vehicles?
Always revisit and rework your model. Often the best version will only come about by tinkering and modifying it until you can't do anymore to it.

What is your favorite brick?
That's a hard one! So many cool parts are released every year. My favorite right now is the 1x1 angled bracket, because it opens up new possibilities.

If you could build any vehicle in the world, what would it be?
A time machine. It would be great to visit the future and see what it holds!

Building instructions

Here's how to make the mini jet, steam train, longship, and excavator that come with this book. Start off your collection of fun vehicle builds with these four models. What will you build next?

Jet

1

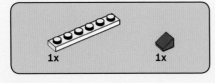

2

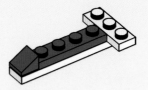

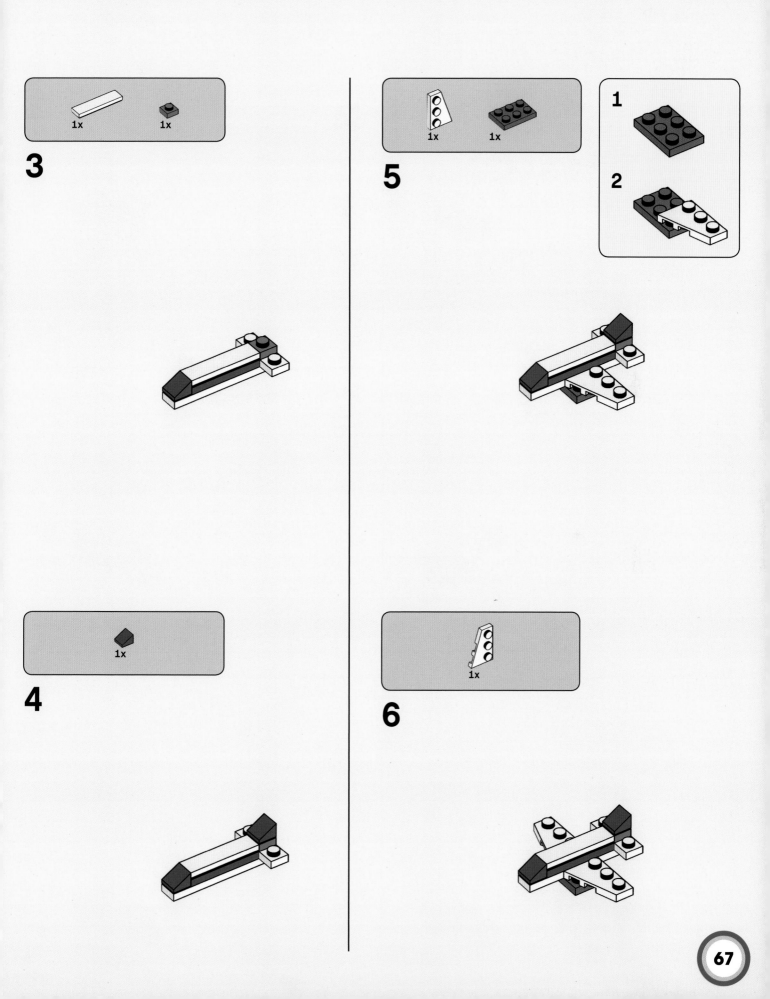

3

1x   1x

4

1x

5

1   2

1x   1x

6

1x

Steam train

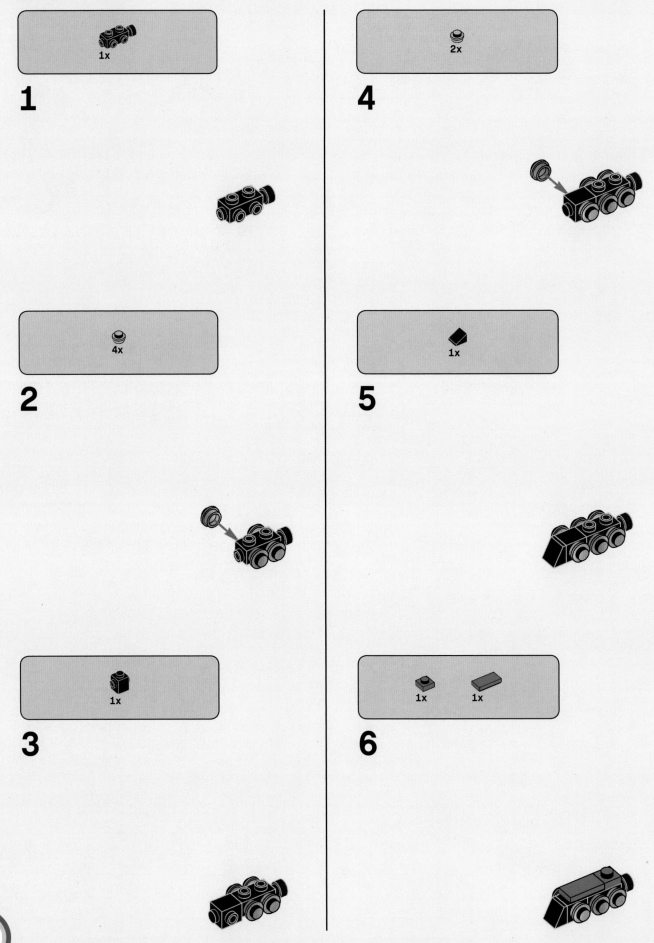

7

1x

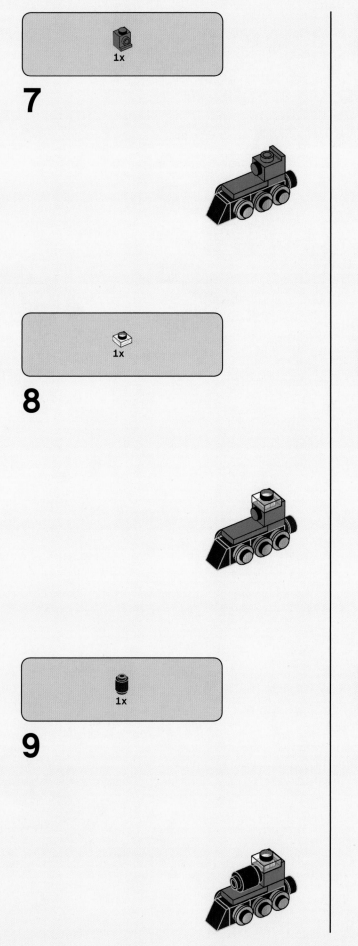

8

1x

9

1x

10

1x 1x

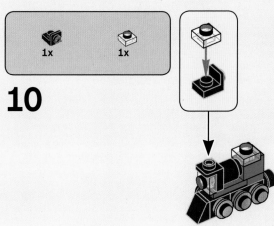

11

1x

12

1x

Longship

1

2

3

4

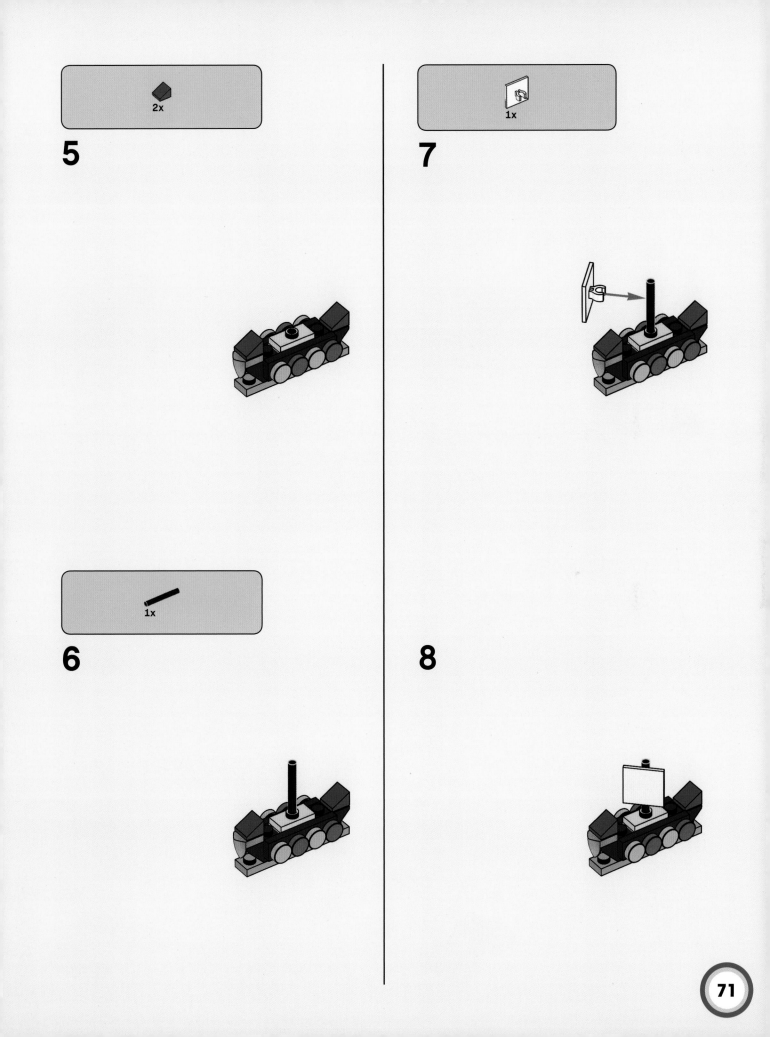

5

2x

6

1x

7

1x

8

Excavator

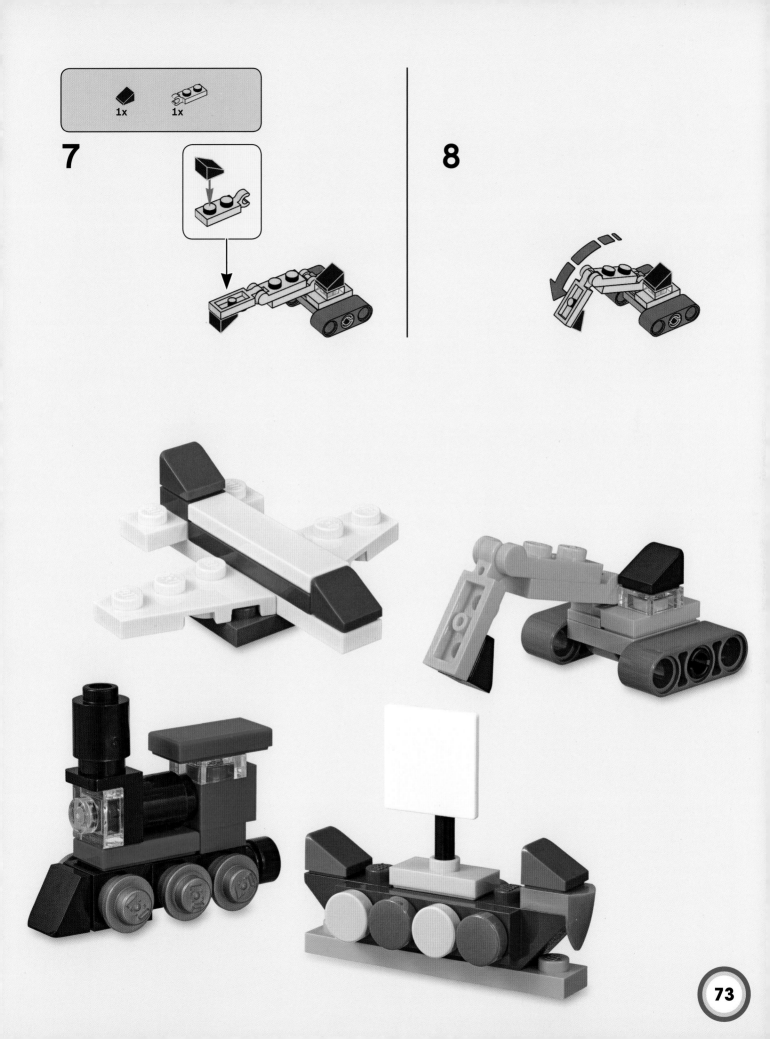

7

1x 1x

8

Glossary

Propeller
tilts up
and down

Blimp

Pickup
truck bed ...

Monster truck

Bumper
guard

ROGER
THAT!

Aluminum
A lightweight, silver-colored metal. Aluminum is commonly used to make vehicles.

Asteroid
A small, rocky object that orbits the Sun.

Bow
The forward end of a vessel, such as a ship.

Bridge
The area of a ship from which the captain or crew can navigate.

Capsize
To turn over in water.

Carbon fiber
A very strong, lightweight material that is often used to make vehicles, such as cars and airplanes.

Continuous track
A continuous band of track plates or treads that is driven by two or more wheels. The track helps vehicles, such as crawler cranes, grip all types of ground.

Conveyor belt
A continuous moving band of material, such as rubber, that transports objects from one place to another.

Diesel
A type of heavy oil that is used as fuel in some kinds of engines.

Ducted fan
A propeller housed inside a tube called a duct.

Efficient
To perform a function or job without wasting much effort and time.

Energy
The power that makes something, such as an engine, work.

Envelope
The fabric of a hot air balloon, which has an opening at the bottom and is attached to the basket of the balloon.

Equipment
A set of necessary objects or tools that are used for a specific purpose or job.

Fiberglass
A type of material made from plastic and glass fibers. Fiberglass is sometimes used to make vehicles.

Force
The pull or push on an object that causes it to move, slow down, or stay in place.

Fuselage
The main body of an aircraft, such as that of an airplane.

Gasoline
A type of lightweight oil that is used as fuel in some kinds of engines.

Passenger
door

Fuselage

Single propeller

Monoplane

Early helicopter

Blade

Tail light

Wheels for landing

Seaplane

Red port light

Gravity
The force that pulls objects toward the center of the Earth. Gravity keeps objects from floating away.

Harbor
An area of water, often with piers or jetties, where boats can moor or dock.

Hull
The main body of a ship or other vessel. The hull is made up of the bottom, sides, and deck of a ship.

Hydraulic
A type of mechanical system that uses fluid to operate. Excavators and dump trucks use hydraulics to move parts of their machinery.

Maneuver
To move with skill and with care.

Monoplane
An airplane with only one set of wings.

Orbit
To travel around something. The Earth orbits the Sun.

Port
The left side of a vessel, such as a ship, when facing forward.

Pressure
The physical force put on an object by another object.

Rechargeable battery
A battery that can be charged with electricity more than once in order to give the battery energy again.

Solar system
The Sun and the eight planets, asteroids, comets, and other smaller bodies that orbit it.

Streamlined
An object that is designed to move very quickly through air or water.

Suspension
The system of tires, shock absorbers, and springs that connects a vehicle to its wheels. It helps to reduce the uncomfortable effects of bumps on the road.

Technology
Tools and devices that help people to do things, such as travel around, more easily.

Vehicle
An object that transports people, animals, or goods from one place to another.

Watertight
Sealed tightly so that no water can pass through.

MAYBE I SHOULD HAVE GONE BY TRAIN...

Hood

Corridor connector

High-speed train

Personal watercraft

Index

Passenger space plane

Passenger cabin

Main rotor hub

Rescue helicopter

Unmanned aerial vehicle

Battery

School bus

Door

Pilot

Unmanned aerial vehicle controller

Removable tail

Flying car

Safety helmet

I CAN'T DECIDE WHICH PAGE TO LAND ON!

Personal flyer

Mast

Fishing trawler

Anchor